A
A
D

NEW YORK

edited by Patrice Farameh

Art Architecture Design

teNeues

ART

ARCHITECTURE

DESIGN

NEW YORK

A A D

Content

Patrice Farameh

All that has to do with art, architecture and design has an address in New York City. New York is a living, breathing, pulsating place that opens itself up to all that is possible; everything here is more than just unique, it feels different. Even though it is one of the most easily recognizable cityscapes on the planet, it is also the most difficult to define. The only way to get a look inside the soul of the city is to dwell deep into its cultural and architectural landscape. Design and art permeates every corner in New York, all shaped through the past and present, with a glimpse into the future. Whether it is constructed in steel or painted on canvas, the ever-changing concepts in design outwardly mirror the constantly shifting aesthetics of not only New York and its residents, but of humanity as a whole.

Alles, was mit Kunst, Architektur und Design verbunden ist, hat auch eine New Yorker Adresse. New York ist ein lebendiger, pulsierender Ort, der sich allen Möglichkeiten gegenüber offen zeigt: Hier ist alles nicht nur einmalig, sondern fühlt sich außerdem andersartig an. Und obwohl die Stadt mit ihren Gebäuden einen sehr hohen Wiedererkennungswert hat, lässt sie sich dennoch nur schwer beschreiben. Um einen Blick in die Seele der Stadt werfen zu können, muss man tief in ihre Kultur- und Architekturlandschaft eintauchen. In New York trifft man einfach überall auf Design und Kunst, immer geprägt von Vergangenheit und Gegenwart, auch die Zukunft lässt sich schon erahnen. Ob Stahlkonstruktion oder Leinwandgemälde, die ständig wechselnden Designkonzepte spiegeln nicht nur die im stetigen Wandel befindliche Ästhetik der Stadt New York und ihrer Bewohner wider, sondern auch die der gesamten Menschheit.

«Tout ce qui a trait à l'art, à l'architecture et au design est en vitrine à New York. C'est un lieu vivant, respirant, dont le cœur battant est ouvert à tous les possibles; tout ici est plus qu'unique car on sent la différence. Si ce décor urbain est l'un des plus connus de la planète, il est aussi le plus difficile à définir. La seule façon de sonder l'âme de cette ville consiste à s'installer dans son paysage culturel et architectural. L'art et le design y imprègnent chaque coin de rue, que le passé et le présent ont façonné, et qui donne un aperçu de l'avenir. Des constructions en acier aux peintures sur toile, les concepts toujours changeant de la conception proposent un reflet de l'esthétique en constante évolution, non seulement de New York et de ses habitants, mais encore de l'humanité toute entière.

Todo lo que tiene que ver con el arte, la arquitectura y el diseño se encuentra en Nueva York. Es una ciudad viva, vibrante, que respira y está abierta a todas las posibilidades; aquí las cosas no son sólo únicas, se sienten de manera distinta. A pesar de ser uno de los paisajes urbanos más fácilmente reconocibles del planeta, también es el más difícil de definir. La única forma de echar un vistazo dentro del alma de la ciudad es vivir profundamente su paisaje cultural y arquitectónico. Diseño y arte impregnan cada rincón de Nueva York, formados todos a través del pasado y del presente, vislumbrando el futuro. Ya sea en acero o sobre lienzos, los siempre cambiantes conceptos en diseño reflejan hacia el exterior los constantes cambios estéticos, no sólo de Nueva York y sus residentes, sino de la humanidad en su conjunto.

ART

A

Considered one of the cultural capitals of the world, it is no surprise that New York City is home to over 80 museums and hundreds of galleries. The anthology of art that has been painstakingly assembled for almost four hundred years on the island of Manhattan is as integral a part of the city as any other aspect of New York life. Whether it be world renowned collections of art found in any of the venerable institutions along the famed Museum Mile to the daring art ventures in the vibrant gallery scene in Chelsea, New York City is the perfect place to challenge those hungry for a variety of first class art. From the modern extensions to classical museums to the new venues erected exclusively for the recent contemporary arts movement; from world class art fairs such as the Armory Show and the Whitney Biennial presenting the newest contemporary works from around the world, there is not a city that can surpass New York in the terms of showcasing arts in all mediums and cultivating those yet to be revealed.

New York zählt zu den Kulturhauptstädten der Welt und so verwundert es nicht, dass die Stadt über 80 Museen und mehrere Hundert Galerien zu bieten hat. Die Kunstwerke, die auf der Insel Manhattan im Verlauf der letzten knapp 400 Jahre sorgfältig zusammengetragen wurden, gehören ebenso untrennbar zur Stadt, wie auch jeder andere Aspekt des New Yorker Lebens. Angefangen bei den weltberühmten Kunstsammlungen, die in den ehrwürdigen Institutionen entlang der bekannten Museum Mile zu finden sind, bis hin zu den gewagten Kunstprojekten in der Galerieszene in Chelsea – New York bietet gerade all jenen eine Herausforderung, die auf der Suche nach neuer, erstklassiger Kunst sind. Von Erweiterungsbauten an klassische Museen bis hin zu neu errichteten Ausstellungsorten, die einzig im Dienst der jüngsten zeitgenössischen Kunstbewegungen stehen, von Kunstmessen auf Weltniveau, wie zum Beispiel die Armory Show, bis hin zur Whitney Biennale, die allerneuste Werke aus aller Welt ausstellen – in keiner Stadt wird mehr Kunst aus allen Bereichen gezeigt, und keine Stadt pflegt jene Kunst mehr, die es noch zu entdecken gilt.

Vu comme l'une des capitales culturelles du monde, New York est sans surprise le foyer de plus de 80 musées et de centaines de galeries. L'anthologie de l'art soigneusement amassée pendant près de quatre siècles sur Manhattan y est aussi essentielle que tout autre aspect de la vie new-yorkaise. Tant les collections à la renommée mondiale que l'on trouve dans ses vénérables institutions le long du célèbre Museum Mile, que les entreprises artistiques audacieuses de la scène animée des galeries de Chelsea, font de New York City l'endroit idéal pour les fans d'une variété d'œuvres de premier ordre. Des extensions modernes aux musées traditionnels; des lieux nouveaux exclusifs du mouvement des arts contemporains récents, aux foires de l'art de classe mondiale telles que l'Armory Show et la biennale du Whitney qui présentent les œuvres contemporaines les plus récentes du monde entier, pas une ville ne surpasse New York pour la mise en valeur des arts de toute sortes et le soutien à ceux qui restent à découvrir.

Considerada una de las capitales culturales del mundo, no sorprende que Nueva York albergue más de 80 museos y cientos de galerías. La antología de arte laboriosamente reunida durante casi 400 años en la isla de Manhattan es una parte tan integral de la ciudad como cualquier otro aspecto de la vida de Nueva York. Ya se trate de colecciones de arte de renombre mundial en cualquiera de las venerables instituciones a lo largo de la famosa Museum Mile, o de las atrevidas empresas de arte en la vibrante escena de las galerías en Chelsea, Nueva York es el lugar perfecto para poner a prueba a aquellos hambrientos de una variedad de arte de primera clase. De las modernas extensiones, pasando por los museos clásicos, hasta los nuevos lugares erigidos exclusivamente para el reciente movimiento de arte contemporáneo; desde ferias de arte de clase mundial, como el Armory Show y la Whitney Biennial, que presentan los últimos trabajos contemporáneos de todo el mundo, no hay ciudad que pueda superar a Nueva York en términos de exhibir arte en todos los medios y cultivar aquellos que aún no han sido mostrados.

P.S. 1 CONTEMPORARY ART CENTER

P.S. 1 CONTEMPORARY ART CENTER

22-25 Jackson Avenue // Queens
Tel.: +1 718 784 2084
www.ps1.org

Thur–Mon 12 pm to 6 pm
G to 21st St

With more than 50 exhibitions a year devoted to emerging artists and new types of artwork, P.S. 1 strives to be more than just a collecting institution and has become home to some of the most experimental art in the world. As an affiliate of the MoMA, the center is one of the greatest purveyors of modern art with the strength to bring innovative and pioneering artwork to international audiences.

Über 50 Ausstellungen im Jahr, die Nach-wuchskünstlern und neuen Kunstformen gewidmet sind, zeugen davon, dass das P.S.1 mehr sein will als ein reines Museum, sondern weltweit einer der experimentier-freudigsten Kunstschauplätze ist. Dem P.S.1, das an das MoMA angegliedert ist, gelingt es immer wieder, innovative und zukunftsweisende Kunstwerke einem internationalen Publikum zugänglich zu machen.

Avec plus de 50 expositions par an consacrées à des artistes émergents et à de nouvelles formes d'art, le P.S.1 se veut plus qu'une simple institution de collecte d'art. Il abrite certaines des techniques artistiques les plus expérimentales du monde. Affilié au MoMA, le centre est un très grand exposant d'art moderne et a démontré qu'il était capable d'attirer un public international vers l'innovation et les œuvres d'avant-garde.

Con más de 50 exhibiciones anuales de-dicadas a artistas primerizos y nuevos tipos de actividades artísticas, P.S.1 se esfuerza por ser más que una institución coleccionista y ha acabado albergando algunas de las manifestaciones artísticas más experimentales. El centro, afiliado al MoMA, es uno de los mayores proveedo-res de arte moderno con capacidad para presentar piezas innovadoras y pioneras al público internacional.

The Cooper-Hewitt houses a collection of over 250,000 objects that is devoted entirely to the study of contemporary design and hosts the much-anticipated National Design Triennial and the National Design Awards. The Museum's architecture is as appealing as its exhibitions; this former Carnegie mansion was originally finished in 1901 with design elements all nostalgic of the time. The gift shop carries one-of-a-kind decorative objects and an impressive selection of books for anyone interested in the future of design.

Im Cooper-Hewitt befindet sich eine Sammlung von über 250 000 Werken modernen Designs. Es veranstaltet das Museum die beliebte National Design Triennale und vergibt den National Design Award. Die Museumsarchitektur ist ebenso ansprechend wie die Ausstellungen – das ehemalige Carnegie-Gebäude aus dem Jahre 1901 besticht durch seinen zeitgenössischen Gebäudeschmuck. Der Museumsshop bietet einzigartige Dekorationsobjekte und eine beeindruckende Buchauswahl.

Le Cooper-Hewitt abrite une collection de plus de 250 000 objets, entièrement consacrée à l'étude du design contemporain, et accueille la très attendue National Design Triennal et le National Design Awards. Son architecture est aussi attrayante que ses expositions; les éléments design de cette ancienne demeure de Carnegie achevée en 1901 rappellent cette époque. Sa boutique comporte des objets décoratifs uniques en leur genre ainsi qu'une sélection impressionnante de livres.

El Cooper-Hewitt acoge una colección de más de 250 000 piezas dedicada por completo al estudio del diseño contemporáneo; en él se conceden los muy anticipados National Design Triennial y National Design Awards. La arquitectura del museo resulta tan atractiva como sus exposiciones; la antigua mansión Carnegie fue concluida en 1901 y su diseño es hijo de su tiempo. La tienda del museo cuenta con objetos de decoración exclusivos y un asombroso fondo bibliográfico.

COOPER-HEWITT DESIGN MUSEUM

2 East 91st Street // Upper East Side
Tel.: +1 212 849 8400
www.cooperhewitt.org
www.cooperhewittshop.org

Mon–Fri 10 am to 5 pm, Sat 10 am to 6 pm,
Sun 11 am to 6 pm
4, 5, 6 to 86th St or 6 to 96th St

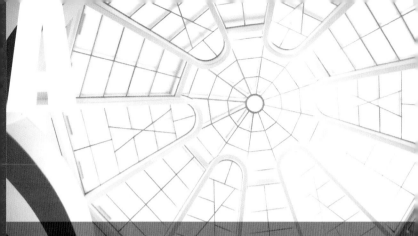

Designed by Frank Lloyd Wright to be a space as exciting and inspiring as the art it holds, this museum is one of the most significant architectural icons of the 20th century. With its unique multi-level structure, one can see art from different distances and heights, allowing the viewer multiple perspectives. Founded on early modern masterpieces, today the museum continues to increase its collection of forward-thinking contemporary pieces from the last century and beyond.

Das von Frank Lloyd Wright entworfene Museum, das ebenso aufregend und inspirierend sein sollte wie die Kunst, die es beherbergt, ist eine der bedeutendsten Architekturikonen des 20. Jahrhunderts. Der einzigartige Bau mit mehreren Ebenen erlaubt dem Besucher eine Vielzahl an Perspektiven, Kunstwerke aus unterschiedlichen Entfernungen und Höhen zu betrachten. Den Grundstein der Sammlung legten die Meisterwerke der Klassischen Moderne – heute wird das Museum ständig um innovative Werke des 20. und 21. Jahrhunderts erweitert.

Conçu par Frank Lloyd Wright pour être un espace aussi impressionnant et inspirant que les œuvres qu'il contient, ce musée est l'un des plus importants symboles de l'architecture du XXᵉ siècle. Sa structure multi-niveaux unique offre de multiples perspectives au spectateur depuis des hauteurs et distances diverses. Fondé pour accueillir les premiers chefs-d'œuvre modernes, le musée continue aujourd'hui d'augmenter sa collection d'œuvres d'avant-garde depuis le siècle dernier jusqu'à aujourd'huipériodes plus anciennes.

Diseñado por Frank Lloyd Wright para ser un espacio tan atractivo e inspirador como el arte que alberga, el museo es uno de los principales iconos arquitectónicos del siglo XX. Su inconfundible estructura a varios niveles permiten contemplar el arte desde distancias y alturas distintas, con lo que el espectador gana diferentes perspectivas. Fundado sobre la base de tempranas obras maestras del arte moderno, el museo continúa ampliando en la actualidad su colección de piezas del siglo pasado y el actual.

SOLOMON
R. GUGGENHEIM MUSEUM

1071 Fifth Avenue // Upper East Side
Tel.: +1 212 423 3500
www.guggenheim.org

Sun–Wed 10 am to 5.45 pm, Fri 10 am to 5.45 pm,
Sat 10 am to 7.45 pm
4, 5, 6 to 86th St

The two exhibition floors in this elegant mansion are entirely dedicated to German and Austrian fine and decorative arts and celebrates illustrious artistic movements and artists of the early 20th century such as Gustav Klimt, Egon Schiele or Oskar Kokoschka. Located alongside the renowned Museum Mile, Neue Galerie New York is a beautifully restored Beaux Arts landmark building that includes 4,300 sq. ft. of exhibition space, a wood-paneled book and design store, and two Viennese cafés.

Auf zwei Stockwerken werden in diesem eleganten Gebäude Kunst und Kunsthandwerk aus Deutschland und Österreich gezeigt. Die Galerie hat sich den berühmten Künstlerbewegungen des frühen 20. Jahrhunderts verschrieben – ausgestellt werden Künstler wie Gustav Klimt, Egon Schiele und Oskar Kokoschka. Die Neue Galerie befindet sich auf der Museum Mile in einem stilvoll restaurierten, denkmalgeschützten Beaux Arts-Gebäude mit 400 m² Ausstellungsfläche, einem holzvertäfelten Buchladen und zwei Wiener Cafés.

Les deux étages d'exposition de cette élégante demeure sont entièrement consacrés aux beaux-arts et aux arts décoratifs allemands et autrichiens. Ils célèbrent les mouvements artistiques illustres et les artistes du début du XXe siècle tels que Gustav Klimt, Egon Schiele ou Oskar Kokoschka. Situé le long du Museum Mile, la Neue Galerie est un bâtiment historique de style Beaux-arts magnifiquement restauré qui comprend 400 m² d'espace d'exposition, une librairie dans un décor de boiseries et deux cafés viennois.

Las dos plantas de exposición de esta elegante mansión están dedicadas por completo a las bellas artes y el arte decorativo alemán y austríaco, y rinde homenaje a ilustres artistas y movimientos de principios del siglo XX como Gustav Klimt, Egon Schiele o Oskar Kokoschka. Sita en la prestigiosa Museum Mile, la Neue Galerie es un hermoso edificio restaurado de estilo Beaux Arts que cuenta con 400 m² de salas de exposición, una librería con paneles de madera y dos cafés vieneses.

NEUE GALERIE NEW YORK MUSEUM FOR GERMAN AND AUSTRIAN ART

1048 Fifth Avenue // Upper East Side
Tel.: +1 212 628 6200
www.neuegalerie.org

Thur–Mon 11 am to 6 pm
B, C, 4, 5, 6 to 86th St

METROPOLITAN MUSEUM OF ART

METROPOLITAN MUSEUM OF ART

1000 Fifth Avenue // Upper East Side
Tel.: +1 212 535 7710
www.metmuseum.org

Tue–Thur 9.30 am to 5.30 pm, Fri–Sat 9.30 am to 9 pm,
Sun 9.30 am to 5.30 pm
4, 5, 6 to 86th St or 6 to 77th St

With 17 curatorial departments dedicated to establishing and maintaining an art collection that includes myriad mediums from every single era in recorded time, the Met is truly a universal museum that holds one of the largest cultural institutions in the world. With over two million objects of art spanning five thousand years of world culture, the museum houses the best collection of works for comparison, contemplation and study for nearly five million visitors per year.

Mit 17 Abteilungen, die sich dem Aufbau und Pflege der Sammlung unterschiedlichster Kunstgegenstände sämtlicher Epochen widmen, ist das Metropolitan Museum of Art ein echtes Universalmuseum und eine der größten Kulturinstitutionen weltweit. Das Museum besitzt über zwei Millionen Objekte aus 5 000 Jahren Weltkulturgeschichte – und zieht jährlich fast fünf Millionen Besucher an, die die Werke betrachten, vergleichen und verstehen möchten.

Ses 17 départements de conservation se consacrent à l'entretien d'une collection qui comprend une myriade de modes d'expressions provenant de toutes les époques de l'histoire. Le Met est un vrai musée universel et constitue l'une des plus grandes institutions culturelles du monde. Avec plus de deux millions d'objets d'art, le musée abrite une collection idéale pour des visiteurs – près de cinq millions par an – qui veulent comparer, étudier ou simplement contempler ces œuvres.

Gracias a sus 17 departamentos dedicados a la creación y conservación de una colección de arte que abarca infinidad de medios de todas y cada una de las eras de la Historia humana, el Met es sencillamente un museo universal y una de las principales instituciones culturales del mundo. Con sus más de dos millones de objetos de arte, el museo alberga la mejor colección de obras para la comparación, la contemplación y el estudio al que se entregan sus casi cinco millones de visitantes anuales.

WHITNEY MUSEUM OF AMERICAN ART

WHITNEY MUSEUM OF AMERICAN ART

945 Madison Avenue // Upper East Side
Tel.: +1 212 570 3600
www.whitney.org

Wed–Thur 11 am to 6 pm, Fri 1 pm to 9 pm,
Sat–Sun 11 am to 6 pm
6 to 77th St

Founded in 1931 with the mission to preserve and present the progression of art from the U.S., the Whitney became the first museum to dedicate its space solely to the works of living American artists. Today it houses the most comprehensive collection of 20th century and contemporary American art in the nation. Aside from its permanent collection of 18,000 pieces, the Biennial is the museum's signature exhibition that focuses on works of lesser-known living artists.

Seit der Gründung im Jahr 1931 dokumentiert das Museum die Entwicklung der Kunst aus den USA. Damit war es die erste Institution, die sich ausschließlich den Arbeiten lebender amerikanischer Künstler widmete. Noch heute nennt das Whitney Museum die umfangreichste Sammlung amerikanischer Kunst des 20. Jahrhunderts und der Gegenwart sein Eigen. Neben der 18 000 Werke umfassenden Dauerausstellung ist das Museum für die Whitney Biennale bekannt, die besonders unbekannteren lebenden Künstlern ein Forum bietet.

Fondé en 1931 avec la mission de préserver et d'exposer l'évolution de l'art américain, ce musée est devenu le premier à se consacrer uniquement aux œuvres d'artistes américains vivants. Aujourd'hui, il abrite la collection la plus complète du XXᵉ siècle et de l'art contemporain sur le territoire américain. Outre sa collection permanente de 18 000 œuvres, le Whitney est aussi connu pour son exposition phare, une biennale qui a pour objet la production d'artistes vivants moins connus.

Fundado en 1931 con el objetivo de preservar y presentar la evolución del arte estadounidense, el Whitney se convirtió en el primer museo que dedicó sus salas en exclusiva a la obra de artistas americanos contemporáneos y vivos. En la actualidad alberga la más extensa colección de arte estadounidense contemporáneo y del siglo XX. Además de su colección permanente de 18 000 piezas, el museo cuenta con una destacada exposición bienal centrada en la obra de artistas poco conocidos.

MUSEUM OF ARTS AND DESIGN

2 Columbus Circle // Midtown
Tel.: +1 212 299 7777
www.madmuseum.org

Tue–Sun 11 am to 6 pm, Thur 11 am to 9 pm
1, A, B, C, D to Columbus Circle

TOTALLY RAD
KARIM RASHID DOES RADIATORS

The Museum of Arts and Design has served as an internationally acclaimed resource center dedicated for nearly half a century to the collection, exhibition and preservation of contemporary craft. Designed by architect Brad Cloepfil, the new building at the revived Columbus Circle is a work of art on its own. Clad with custom-made tiles, this twelve-story building has over 54,000-sq-ft of space for exhibitions and educational programs, including a restaurant with views over Central Park and a 150-seat theater.

Seit fast 50 Jahren hat sich das internatio-nal bekannte Museum of Arts and Design der Sammlung, Ausstellung und Erhaltung zeitgenössischen Kunstgewerbes ver-schrieben. Der mit Architekt Brad Cloepfil entworfene Neubau am wiederbelebten Columbus Circle ist an sich schon ein Kunst-werk mit seinen eigens gefertigten Kacheln an der Außenfassade. Auf zwölf Stockwer-ke und über 5 000 m² bietet es Platz für Ausstellungen und Bildungsangebote, ein Restaurant mit Blick über den Central Park und ein Auditorium mit 150 Plätzen.

Le musée a servi pendant près d'un de-mi-siècle de centre de ressources mondia-lement reconnu, consacré à la collecte, à l'exposition et à la conservation d'oeuvres artisanales contemporaines. Dessiné par l'architecte Brad Cloepfil, ce nouveau bâti-ment de Columbus Circle est lui-même une œuvre d'art. Revêtu de tuiles faites sur me-sure, ses douze étages contiennent plus de 5 000 m² d'espace d'exposition et d'activi-tés éducatives, un restaurant avec vue sur Central Park et un théâtre de 150 places.

El museo lleva casi medio siglo de exis-tencia como centro internacionalmente reconocido de colección, exposición y con-servación de creaciones contemporáneas. Creado en colaboración con el arquitecto Brad Cloepfil, el nuevo edificio del Colum-bus Circle es una obra de arte en sí mismo. Recubiertas con baldosas especiales, las doce plantas de este edificio ofrecen 5 000 m² para exposiciones y programas educa-tivos, además de albergar un restaurante con vistas sobre Central Park y un teatro de 150 plazas.

JULIAN SCHNAB

Julian Schnabel is one of America's most illustrious and respected living art superstars. His first show at the famed Mary Boone Gallery launched his career as an artist over two decades ago. Known for his trademark paintings on gigantic canvases with unusual surface materials such as broken pottery and animal hides, this highly controversial and outspoken artist is a major force in the contemporary art market today, and his artwork is displayed in museums and galleries throughout the world. Yearning to explore more creative outlets, Schnabel established himself as a successful filmmaker by directing artistic biographies about people who also define their lives through their art, such as the award-winning The Diving Bell and the Butterfly. He has also made his mark on the New York architectural landscape by developing Palazzo Chupi, a soaring pink 17-story residence in the West Village.

Julian Schnabel ist einer der berühmtesten und angesehensten Künstler Amerikas. Seine Karriere begann vor über 20 Jahren mit seiner ersten Ausstellung in der legendären Mary Boone Gallery. Übergroße Gemälde, bei denen er ungewöhnliche Materialien – Tonscherben und Tierhaut – einsetzt, gelten als sein Markenzeichen. Mit seinen kontroversen Arbeiten und seiner prägnanten Persönlichkeit hat er sich als wichtige Größe auf dem Markt für zeitgenössische Kunst etabliert, seine Werke finden sich weltweit in Museen und Galerien. Bei der Suche nach weiteren kreativen Betätigungsfeldern wurde Schnabel zum erfolgreichen Filmemacher und realisierte künstlerische Biografien über Menschen, die ihr Leben durch ihre Kunst definieren – so entstand der preisgekrönte Film „Schmetterling und Taucherglocke". Mit dem Bau des Palazzo Chupi, einem pinken 17-stöckiges Wohnhaus im West Village, drückte er auch der New Yorker Architekturlandschaft seinen Stempel auf.

EL

Julian Schnabel est une star de l'art américain des plus illustres et respectées encore en vie. Sa première exposition à la célèbre Mary Boone Gallery a lancé sa carrière en tant qu'artiste il y a plus de deux décennies. Connu pour son style de peinture sur d'immenses support incorporant des matériaux aux textures inhabituelles comme la terre cuite et les peaux d'animaux, cet artiste au francparler controversé est une force majeure du marché de l'art contemporain actuel, et ses œuvres peuplent nombre de musées et galeries du monde. Schnabel désire explorer d'autres modes d'expression et a confirmé son talent de cinéaste en filmant la biographie artistique de gens se définissant dans l'art, telle son œuvre primée Le scaphandre et le papillon. Le paysage architectural new-yorkais porte aussi son empreinte, le Palazzo Chupi, une résidence rose élancée de 17 étages dans le West Village.

Julian Schnabel es una de los más ilustres y respetadas luminarias en el mundo del arte actual. Su primera exposición en la galería Mary Boone supuso el trampolín para su carrera, hace ahora dos décadas. Conocido por sus característicos lienzos de enormes dimensiones tratados con materiales poco habituales (fragmentos de loza rota, pieles de animales) el artista, siempre controvertido y locuaz, es una de las fuerzas motrices del mercado contemporáneo del arte, y su obra se expone en museos y galerías de todo el mundo. Ansioso por explorar nuevas vías a través de las cuales canalizar su creatividad, Schnabel es también un prestigioso cineasta, que dirige biografías artísticas de personas que definen sus vidas a través de su arte, como sucede en la galardonada La escafandra y la mariposa. Asimismo ha dejado huella en el panorama arquitectónico neoyorquino con el Palazzo Chupi, un imponente edificio residencial rosado de 17 plantas en el West Village.

A

MUSEUM OF MODERN ART

Since its humble opening in 1929 which featured only nine piecesworks, the MoMA has expanded its permanent collection to more than 150,000 pieces of art and over 22,000 films, and itself is an architectural wonder. The building's $425 million face-lift by Yoshio Taniguchi inspires awe with its contemporary spaces, labyrinth of glass walkways and 110-ft atrium entrance. Dining options include the award-winning restaurant The Modern and the MoMA Store offers patrons a carefully curated selection of books and design objects.

Seit dem bescheidenen Anfang im Jahr 1929 mit gerade mal neun Werken hat das MoMA seine Sammlung auf über 150 000 Kunstwerke und 22 000 Filme erweitert. Auch das Museum selbst ist ein architektonisches Meisterwerk. Seit der Umgestaltung durch Yoshio Taniguchi beeindruckt das Gebäude mit modernen Räumen, einem Labyrinth aus Glasgängen und einem 34 m hohen Atrium. Das preisgekrönte Restaurant The Modern lädt zum Dinieren ein und der MoMA Store bietet sorgfältig ausgewählte Bücher und Designobjekte.

The Broken Kilometer/Barbara & Friedrich Ackers

Depuis ses humbles débuts avec neuf objets d'art en 1929, le MoMA a élargi sa collection permanente à plus de 150 000 œuvres et à plus de 22 000 films. Il est lui-même une merveille architecturale et sa réfection par Yoshio Taniguchi, dont les espaces contemporains, le cheminement labyrinthique de verre et l'atrium de l'entrée d'une hauteur de 34 m inspirent l'admiration. On peut y dîner au The Modern, et la MoMA Store offre aux visiteurs une sélection soigneusement organisée de livres et d'objets design.

Desde su modesta inauguración en 1929 con apenas nueve piezas, el MoMA ha ampliado su colección permanente y abarca hoy más de 150 000 obras de arte y 22 000 filmaciones, y es en sí mismo una maravilla arquitectónica. La remodelación del edificio acometida por Yoshio Taniguchi asombra con espacios contemporáneos, laberintos de pasarelas de cristal y un atrio de 34 m de alto. Además del prestigioso restaurante The Modern, la MoMA Store ofrece una cuidada selección de libros y objetos de diseño.

MUSEUM OF MODERN ART

11 West 53 Street // Midtown
Tel.: +1 212 708 9400
www.moma.org

Mon 10.30 am to 5.30 pm, Wed–Thur 10.30 am to 5.30 pm,
Fri 10.30 am to 8 pm, Sat–Sun 10.30 am to 5.30 pm
E, V to 53rd St and Fifth Ave or B, D, F, M to 47-50 St / Rockefeller Center

MOMA STORE

11 West 53 Street // Midtown
Tel.: +1 212 708 9400
www.moma.org

Sat–Thur 9.30 am to 6.30 pm

THE MODERN RESTAURANT

9 West 53 Street // Midtown
Tel.: +1 212 333 1220
www.themodernnyc.com

Mon–Fri noon to 2 pm (lunch),
Mon–Thur 5.30 pm to 10.30 pm,
Fri–Sat 5.30 pm to 11 pm (dinner)

Founded in 1974 with the mission to keep the legacy of "concerned photography" alive, the ICP serves as both a museum and school committed to showcasing the possibilities of photography through exhibition and education. Their collection spans the history of photography and contains more than 100,000 original prints, with an emphasis on documentary photography from the 1930s to 1990s. Their complementary store carries a wide array of photography books. The ICP also presents the Infinity Awards each year.

Seit der Gründung im Jahr 1974 hat das ICP den Auftrag, das Vermächtnis der engagierten Fotografie zu bewahren. Das ICP ist Museum und Schule zugleich: Ausstellungen und Bildungsangebote verdeutlichen die Vielfältigkeit der Fotografie. Die Sammlung spiegelt die Geschichte der Fotografie wider und umfasst über 100 000 Originalabzüge mit Schwerpunkt auf der Dokumentationsfotografie der 1930er bis 1990er Jahre. Der angeschlossene Museumsshop bietet eine große Auswahl an Fotobänden.

Fondée en 1974 avec la mission de conserver vivant l'héritage de la « photo engagée », le ICP sert à la fois de musée et d'école et s'engage à mettre en valeur le potentiel de la photographie par le biais de l'enseignement et de l'exposition. Sa collection couvre l'histoire de la photographie et contient plus de 100 000 épreuves originales dont une grande partie de photos documentaires des années 1930 aux années 1990. Sa librairie propose un vaste choix de livres traitant de la photographie.

Fundado en 1974 para mantener con vida el legado de la "fotografía comprometida", el ICP sirve a un tiempo como museo y escuela dedicada a demostrar las posibilidades de la fotografía a través de la educación. Su colección abarca toda la historia de la fotografía y dispone de más de 100 000 imágenes originales, con especial énfasis en la fotografía documental entre las décadas de 1930 y 1990. En la tienda del museo disponen de una amplia selección de libros de fotografía.

photos by Paul Warchol

INTERNATIONAL CENTER OF PHOTOGRAPHY

1133 Avenue of the Americas // Midtown
Tel.: +1 212 857 0000
www.icp.org

Tue–Thur 10 am to 6 pm, Fri 10 am to 8 pm,
Sat–Sun 10 am to 6 pm
B, D, F, M, 7 to 42nd St / Bryant Park

With eight locations worldwide—three in Manhattan alone—this gallery is dedicated to contemporary art and considered one of the few galleries in the world that deservedly competes with museums. Owned by Larry Gagosian, one of the most powerful people in the contemporary art world, it has been said that having a show at any of his galleries is a sure sign that one has reached notoriety as an artist.

Die Galerie hat sich der zeitgenössischen Kunst verschrieben und ist mit ihren acht Filialen weltweit – allein drei davon in Manhattan – eine der wenigen Galerien der Welt, die die Konkurrenz mit Museen nicht zu scheuen braucht. Ihr Besitzer Larry Gagosian ist einer der einflussreichsten Menschen der zeitgenössischen Kunstwelt. Man sagt, ein sicheres Zeichen, es als Künstler geschafft zu haben, sei es, in einer seiner Galerien ausgestellt zu haben.

La Gagosian, constituée de huit galeries dans le monde dont trois à Manhattan, se consacre à l'art contemporain et reste considérée comme l'une des rares dans le monde à pouvoir concurrencer les musées. Elle appartient à Larry Gagosian, une personnalité influente du monde de l'art contemporain. Le fait d'être exposé dans l'une de ses galeries a été décrit comme une preuve pour tout artiste d'avoir atteint la notoriété.

Con sus ocho locales en todo el mundo (tres de ellos en Manhattan), esta galería concentrada en el arte contemporáneo pasa por ser una de las pocas capaz de equipararse con los museos. Propiedad de Larry Gagosian, uno de las personas más poderosas en el mundo del arte contemporáneo, de la galería se ha dicho que exponer en ella es signo inequívoco de que el artista ha llegado a lo más alto.

GAGOSIAN GALLERY

980 Madison Avenue // Upper East Side
Tel.: +1 212 744 2313
Mon–Sat 10 am to 6 pm
Shop at 988 Madison Avenue
Tel.: +1 212 744 9200

Mon–Sat 10 am to 6 pm
6 to 77th St

522 West 21st Street // Chelsea
Tel.: +1 212 741 1717
555 West 24th Street
Tel.: +1 212 741 1111

Mon–Sat 10 am to 6 pm
C, E to 23rd St
www.gagosian.com

MATTHEW MARKS GALLERY

523 West 24th Street, 522 and 526 West 22nd Street // Chelsea
Tel.: +1 212 243 0200
www.matthewmarks.com

Tue–Sat 11 am to 6 pm
C, E to 23rd St

Matthew Marks has earned a solid reputation for having a keen sense of A-list contemporary and modern art. Marks is described by his peers as selfless in his pursuits to promote artists and their work to the general public through various exhibitions and carefully edited catalogues, With three locations in Chelsea and 26 American and European artists in its exclusive listing, the gallery is one of the prime exhibition spaces in the country.

Matthew Marks' guter Ruf beruht auf seinem ausgeprägten Sinn für die beste zeitgenössische und moderne Kunst und seiner selbstlosen Förderung von Künstlern und deren Arbeiten. Mit vielen Ausstellungen und sorgfältig aufbereiteten Katalogen trägt er dazu bei, diese der breiteren Öffentlichkeit zugänglich zu machen. Die Galerie hat drei Standorte in Chelsea und vertritt 26 amerikanische und europäische Künstler exklusiv – sie ist somit eines der führenden Ausstellungsorte des Landes.

Matthew Marks a acquis une réputation solide pour son sens aigu de LA liste des œuvres d'art contemporaines et modernes. Marks est décrit par ses pairs comme désintéressé dans ses activités visant à promouvoir les artistes et leur travail auprès du grand public par le biais d'expositions variées et de catalogues édités avec soin. Grâce à trois adresses dans le quartier de Chelsea et à 26 artistes américains et européens exclusives, la galerie est l'un des espaces d'exposition de choix dans le pays.

Matthew Marks se ha granjeado una sólida reputación por su olfato para reconocer el mejor arte contemporáneo y moderno. Sus socios y compañeros subrayan el altruismo de Marks en la promoción de artistas y su obra a través de diversas exposiciones y catálogos cuidadosamente editados. Con sus tres locales en Chelsea y 26 artistas americanos y europeos fichados en exclusiva, la galería es uno de los principales espacios de exposición del país.

Since its founding over two decades ago, the Gladstone Gallery has specialized in showcasing some of the best work in contemporary art in the city. The gallery also represents 35 artists who work with different ranges of media aside from just paintings and sculpture, including video, film, installation, and photography.

Seit der Gründung vor über 20 Jahren hat sich die Gladstone Gallery auf das Ausstellen einiger der besten Werke der zeitgenössischen Kunst in der Stadt spezialisiert. Außerdem vertritt die Galerie 35 Künstler, die neben Malerei und Bildhauerei mit einer breiten Palette unterschiedlicher Medien arbeiten, wie zum Beispiel mit Video, Film, Installationen und Fotografie.

Depuis sa fondation il y a plus de deux décennies, la galerie Gladstone s'est spécialisée dans la présentation de certaines des meilleures œuvres d'art comtemporain de la ville. La galerie représente aussi 35 artistes qui travaillent avec diverses gammes de supports autres que la peinture et la sculpture, en particulier la vidéo, le cinéma, l'installation et la photographie.

Desde que fuera fundada hace ahora dos décadas, Gladstone Gallery se ha especializado en presentar buena parte del arte contemporáneo más destacado de la ciudad. La galería representa también a 35 artistas que trabajan en todo tipo de medios, más allá de la pintura y la escultura: video, cine, instalaciones y fotografía.

BARBARA GLADSTONE GALLERY

515 West 21st Street // Chelsea
Tel.: +1 212 206 9300
530 West 21st Street // Chelsea
Tel.: +1 212 206 7606
www.gladstonegallery.com

Tue–Sat 10 am to 6 pm
C, E to 23rd St

A

NEW MUSEUM

235 Bowery // Bowery
Tel.: +1 212 219 1222
www.newmuseum.org

Wed, Fri–Sun 11 am to 6 pm, Thur 11 am to 9 pm
J, M to Bowery and F, V to 2nd Ave / Lower East Side

Founded in 1977 as a space dedicated solely to presenting contemporary art from around the globe, the museum also takes an avant-garde approach to its curatorial program by being both an incubator for new ideas and a home for less recognized artists. In 2007 the museum's new home, designed by Pritzker Prize winning architecture duo SANAA, was completed on the Bowery.

Seit dem Gründungsjahr 1977 widmet sich das Museum ausschließlich der zeitgenössischen Kunst aus aller Welt. Auch das kuratorische Programm ist avantgardistisch – das Museum ist sowohl Ort neuer Ideen als auch Ausstellungsort für noch wenig bekannte Künstler. Das neue Museumsgebäude, entworfen vom japanischen Architektenduo SANAA (ausgezeichnet mit dem Pritzker Preis), wurde im Jahr 2007 an der Bowery fertiggestellt.

Ce musée fondé en 1977 comme espace entièrement dédié à la présentation de l'art contemporain du monde entier, présente lui aussi un programme de conservation avant-gardiste, berceau d'idées nouvelles, qui accueille des artistes moins reconnus. La construction du nouveau musée sur le Bowery, conçu par le duo d'architectes SANAA, gagnants du Prix Pritzker, s'est achevée en 2007.

Espacio fundado en 1977 para la presentación en exclusiva de arte contemporáneo de todo el mundo, el museo adoptó también enfoques vanguardistas en su labor curadora, ejerciendo como incubadora de nuevas ideas y refugio de artistas poco conocidos. En 2007 concluyó la construcción de la nueva sede del museo en el Bowery, diseñada por el dúo de arquitectos SANAA, ganador del premio Pritzker.

A hybrid of gallery space and bookstore, both devoted to the art of photography, this stylish minimalist exhibition space on Broome Street features monthly shows by emerging photographers with a wide range of themes. Deemed one the city's most price-worthy galleries for art buyers and novices alike, it also stocks a carefully curated selection of limited and out-of-print editions of the most sought-after photography books at its four other locations: two in Manhattan, one in East Hampton and another on St. Barts.

Ein Hybrid aus Galerie und Buchladen, beides der Fotokunst verschrieben. In diesem minimalistischen Ausstellungsraum an der Broome Street werden im Monatswechsel Ausstellungen unterschiedlichster Nachwuchsfotografen gezeigt. Die Galerie gilt bei erfahrenen und neuen Sammlern als eine der erschwinglichsten der Stadt und hält zudem eine exquisite Auswahl limitierter und vergriffener Fotobücher in den vier Dependancen bereit. Zwei befinden sich in Manhattan, eine in East Hampton und eine auf St. Barths.

Situé sur Broome Street, cet hybride élégant et minimaliste de galerie et de librairie consacrées à la photographie, propose des expositions mensuelles de jeunes photographes sur des thèmes variés. Considérée comme l'une des galeries les plus abordables tant par les collectionneurs que par les curieux, elle détient aussi une sélection d'éditions limitées ou épuisées des livres de photographie qu'elle conserve dans les réserves de ses quatre autres adresses : deux à Manhattan, une dans l'East Hampton et une autre à St Barth.

Mezcla de espacio galerístico y librería, la elegante y minimalista sala de exposición de Broome Street organiza mensualmente muestras de fotógrafos emergentes en torno a un amplio abanico de temas. Considerada una de las galerías más asequibles de la ciudad para marchantes de arte y aficionados, dispone también de una cuidada selección de volúmenes fotográficos de edición limitada o descatalogados en sus cuatro locales: dos en Manhattan, uno en East Hampton y otro en St. Barts.

CLIC BOOKSTORE & GALLERY

255 Centre Street // SoHo
Tel.: +1 212 966 2766
www.clicgallery.com

Mon–Sun 12 pm to 7 pm
6 to Spring St or J, M to Bowery

WILD HORSES OF SABLE ISLAND

13 Crosby Street // SoHo
Tel.: +1 212 219 9622
www.wildhorsesofsableisland.com

Tue–Sat 11 am to 8 pm, Sun 12 pm to 6 pm
N, Q, R, W, 6 to Canal St Station

Much like the wind-swept North Atlantic refuge the Wild Horses of Sable Island inhabit, the high-ceilinged, large, well-lit space that is photographer Roberto Dutesco's SoHo gallery offers dramatic images with solid emotional impact. This quiet, street-level retreat's columned entrance, marked only by a Wild Horses banner, is low-key and inviting with maritime touches. Wild Horses is the city's longest-running, single-themed exhibit.

Die Galerie des Fotografen Roberto Dutesco in SoHo ist hell und großzügig. Hier werden dramatische, emotional berührende Bilder geboten, ähnlich wie der Lebensraum der wilden Pferde von Sable Island, einer von peitschendem Wind geprägten Gegend am Nordatlantik. Der von Säulen umrahmte Eingang, erkennbar nur am Wild-Horses-Banner, ist schlicht, wirkt aber durch den maritimen Touch einladend. Wild Horses ist die am längsten laufende monothematische Ausstellung in New York.

Tout comme la réserve balayée par les vents de l'Atlantique Nord où vivent les chevaux sauvages de Sable Island, ce vaste et clair espace aux plafonds hauts, sert de galerie à SoHo au photographe Roberto Dutesco, et offre des images spectaculaires au fort impact émotionnel. L'entrée à colonnes de cette retraite calme, marquée d'un simple drapeau, est discrète et accueillante avec une certaine touche marine. Wild Horses est l'exposition new-yorkaise mono-thématique ayant duré le plus longtemps.

De forma parecida al refugio que habitan los caballos salvajes de Sable Island en el Atlántico Norte, la espaciosa y luminosa galería del fotógrafo Roberto Dutesco en SoHo ofrece contundentes imágenes de enorme contenido emocional. Tan sólo un cartel anuncia la presencia a nivel de calle del local, que mantiene un perfil bajo pero invitador con toques marítimos. Wild Horses es la exhibición monográfica más longeva de la ciudad.

ARCHIT

A

On an island only 12.5 miles long and 2.5 miles wide, it is amazing that over 5,000 high-rise buildings can be found in Manhattan. While these architectural strongholds are numerous throughout the city, New York is also recognized for setting the most inspiring trends in architecture. A constant influx of world renowned architects and designers are continually making their mark on the most famous skyline in the world, in turn bringing with them the most modern innovations in environmentally conscious construction materials and techniques. Within the confines of the city there exists everything from classic brownstones next to the most futuristic condominium towers, abandoned sites turned into landscaped sculptural gardens, and classical landmark buildings modernized and merged with bold new structures. Even recently built stylish hotels and restaurants have had the power to transform established neighborhoods into a more lively hip scene, proving that the ever-changing inventive spirit of New York the perfect breeding ground for cutting-edge architecture and pioneering concepts.

Es ist erstaunlich, dass auf einer nur 20 km langen und 4 km breiten Insel wie Manhattan über 5 000 Hochhäuser stehen. Und obwohl diese Bollwerke überall in der Stadt zu finden sind, ist New York auch bekannt dafür, die neusten, innovativsten Architekturtrends zu setzen. Immer wieder kommen weltbekannte Architekten und Designer hierher und hinterlassen in der wohl berühmtesten Skyline der Welt ihre Spuren und bringen somit die modernsten Erfindungen im Bereich umweltfreundliche Bautechnologie und Baustoffe nach New York. Innerhalb der Stadtgrenzen finden sich Bauten aller Art: Ziegelsteingebäude stehen neben futuristisch anmutenden Wohntürmen, stillgelegte Areale werden zu Landschaftsgärten und klassische denkmalgeschützte Gebäude werden in kühne Neubauten integriert. Neuen stilvollen Hotels und Restaurants ist es sogar gelungen, in alteingesessenen Stadtvierteln eine lebendigere, trendigere Szene zu etablieren – das zeigt, dass der sich stetig wandelnde erfindungsreiche Geist der Stadt die bestmöglichen Voraussetzungen für innovative Architektur und wegweisende Konzepte bietet.

L'île de Manhattan ne mesurant que 20 km de long par 4 km de large, il est étonnant d'y trouver plus de 5 000 gratte-ciel. Bien que ces bastions de l'architecture y soient nombreux, New York est aussi connue pour lancer les tendances architecturales les plus influentes. Un afflux constant d'architectes et de concepteurs de renommée mondiale marquent le paysage le plus célèbre du monde de leur empreinte, et en remportent les innovations les plus modernes en termes de techniques et de matériaux de construction environnementaux. Tout se côtoie dans l'enceinte de la ville, du grès brun traditionnel aux tours d'habitation les plus futuristes, des sites abandonnés transformés en jardins, aux bâtiments historiques classiques modernisés auxquelles se greffent de nouvelles structures audacieuses. Même les hôtels et restaurants chics récemment construits peuvent transformer des quartiers établis en une scène cool plus vivante, preuve que l'évolution constante de l'esprit inventif new-yorkais est le terreau idéal de l'architecture et des concepts d'avant-garde.

En una isla como Manhattan, de sólo 20 km de largo y 4 km de ancho, es increíble poder encontrar más de 5 000 edificios de gran altura. Mientras estos baluartes arquitectónicos son numerosos en la ciudad, Nueva York también es reconocida por marcar las tendencias arquitectónicas más inspiradoras. Arquitectos y diseñadores de fama mundial acuden sin cesar a la ciudad, dejando continuamente su huella en el perfil más famoso del mundo, portando a su vez con ellos las más modernas innovaciones en materiales de construcción y técnicas respetuosas con el ambiente. Dentro de los confines de la ciudad existe todo, desde casas de ladrillo rojo junto a las más futuristas torres en condominio a solares abandonados convertidos en jardines escultóricos y clásicos edificios históricos modernizados y fusionados con nuevas estructuras. Incluso elegantes hoteles y restaurantes construidos hace poco han tenido el poder de transformar barrios ya establecidos en una escena a la moda más viva, demostrando que el siempre cambiante espíritu inventivo de Nueva York es el terreno perfecto para la arquitectura de vanguardia y los conceptos pioneros.

A

This three-story, all-glass foyer and open area plaza is one of the most utilized venues for intimate concerts at the Lincoln Center for the Performing Arts. Designed initially by Pietro Belluschi in 1969, it has since been transformed into a distraction-free environment by the firm of Diller Scofidio + Renfro. Thanks to a new glass wall in the lobby, the interior of the building appears to seep into the outdoors, creating a relationship between the covered space inside and the public areas outside.

Im Lincoln Center for the Performing Arts ist dieses dreistöckige Glasfoyer mit seiner offenen Plaza einer der meistgenutzten Veranstaltungsorte für kleine Konzerte. Das Gebäude wurde 1969 von Pietro Belluschi geplant und vom Architekturbüro Diller Scofidio + Renfro grundlegend zu einer neuen Spielstätte umgestaltet. Dank seiner gläsernen Lobby entsteht ein Zusammenspiel zwischen dem geschützten Innenraum und öffentlichen Außenraum.

Ce bâtiment de trois étages, avec son hall vitré et son parvis est un lieu fréquemment utilisé pour les concerts intimistes du Lincoln Center for the Performing Arts. Conçu initialement par Pietro Belluschi en 1969, le design de Diller Scofidio + Renfro en a depuis fait un lieu à l'abri des distractions. Grâce à une nouvelle paroi vitrée dans le hall, l'intérieur du bâtiment semble se propager à l'extérieur, créant une relation entre l'espace couvert intérieur et les espaces publics extérieurs.

Las tres plantas de este complejo de vestíbulo acristalado y espacio interior abierto son escenario habitual de intimistas conciertos en el Lincoln Center for the Performing Arts. El diseño original de 1969 de Pietro Belluschi se ha ido transformando en un espacio libre de distracciones concebido por Diller Scofidio + Renfro. El nuevo muro vidriado del vestíbulo establece una relación directa entre el espacio cubierto interior y las áreas públicas externas.

ALICE TULLY HALL

1941 Broadway // Midtown
Tel.: +1 212 671 4050
www.lincolncenter.org

1 to 66th to St Lincoln Center Station

HEARST TOWER

300 West 57th Street // Midtown
www.hearst.com

1, A, B, C, D to 59th St Columbus Circle
or N, Q, R, W to 57th St

This iconic 46-story high-rise by Lord Norman Foster is the first NYC LEED Gold skyscraper in New York City—80 % of its structural steel contains recycled materials, the rain collected on the roof is used for the cooling system and the building uses 26 % less energy than the standard requirement. The original stone facade of this Art Deco design building is a designated landmark that was integrated into its new design, which received the Emporis Skyscraper Award after its completion in 2006.

Dieses 46 Stockwerke hohe Gebäude, entworfen von Lord Norman Foster, ist der erste NYC LEED Gold-zertifizierte Wolkenkratzer in New York – 80 % des Baustahls ist recycelt, das auf dem Dach gesammelte Regenwasser wird zur Kühlung genutzt, und das Gebäude verbraucht 26 % weniger Energie als üblich. Die denkmalgeschützte Steinfassade des Art Deco-Vorgängerbaus wurde in den Entwurf integriert. Der Hearst Tower erhielt im Jahr 2006 den Emporis Skyscraper Award.

Cette tour emblématique de 46 étages conçue par Lord Norman Foster est le premier gratte-ciel de New York à avoir reçu le label environnemental LEED Gold. 80 % de son acier contient des matières recyclées, le toit recueille la pluie pour le système de refroidissement et le bâtiment consomme 26 % moins d'énergie que la norme exigée. La façade originelle en pierre de cette immeuble Art Déco est un repère reconnu qui a été intégré dans le nouveau projet.

El inconfundible edificio de 46 plantas diseñado por Lord Norman Foster es el primer rascacielos neoyorquino en obtener la certificación LEED Gold: un 80 % de su estructura de acero procede de materiales reciclados, la lluvia recogida en la azotea se utiliza en el sistema de refrigeración y el edificio consume un 26 % menos de energía que de los límites obligatorios. La fachada original de piedra, de estilo Art Déco, es un monumento protegido que ha sido integrado en el nuevo diseño.

JOAN WEILL CENTER FOR DANCE
ALVIN AILEY AMERICAN DANCE THEATER

405 West 55th Street // Midtown
Tel.: +1 212 405 9000
www.alvinailey.org

1, A, B, C, D to 59th St Columbus Circle
or N, Q, R, W to 57th St

Considered the city's leading cultural institution focused on architecture, the center hosts a diverse lineup of exhibitions concentrated on the built environment and offers design resources, educational programs and tours for the profession and the public alike. Its incredible 15,000-sq-ft space, designed by Andrew Berman in 2003, has three floors of high ceilings filled with natural light, and includes one of the first geothermal systems in New York.

Das Center gilt als führende Einrichtung für Architektur in New York. Das Angebot umfasst unterschiedlichste Ausstellungen über die gebaute Umwelt. Ebenso gehören Designmaterialien, Bildungsangebote und Führungen für Profis oder Interessierte zum Programm. Im Jahr 2003 konzipierte Andrew Berman diese beeindruckenden, 1 400 m² großen Räumlichkeiten: Tageslicht durchflutet die drei hohen Stockwerke, und als eines der ersten Bauten in New York nutzt es geothermische Energie.

Considéré comme l'institution culturelle phare de la ville pour l'architecture, le centre accueille une programmation diversifiée d'expositions concentrées sur l'environnement bâti et propose des ressources de conception, des programmes éducatifs et des visites pour les professionnels aussi bien que le public. Son espace incroyable de 1 400 m², conçu par Andrew Berman en 2003, comporte trois hauts étages baignés de lumière naturelle, et comprend l'un des premiers systèmes géothermiques de New York.

Considerado la principal institución cultural de la ciudad en cuestiones arquitectónicas, el centro acoge toda una serie de exposiciones centradas en entornos edificados y ofrece recursos de diseño, programas educativos y visitas guiadas para profesionales y aficionados. Sus 1 400 m² de superficie, diseñados por Andrew Berman en 2003, se extienden a lo largo de tres luminosas plantas de altos techos e incluyen uno de los primeros sistemas geotérmicos de Nueva York.

Atop one of the highest buildings in the country, this observation deck recently reopened with an ocean-liner-inspired design after a $75 million renovation. Rising 850 feet above street level at the top of the General Electric Building, the deck allows for spectacular views over the entire city on any of its six levels. The building sits among a complex of 19 buildings in Rockefeller Plaza, unmatched in their artistry and Art Deco style.

Auf einem der höchsten Gebäude der USA befindet sich diese kürzlich wiedereröffnete Dachterrasse. Nach einer 75 Millionen Dollar teuren Runderneuerung erhebt sich die an ein Deck eines Ozeanriesen erinnernde Plattform auf dem Dach des General Electric Gebäudes. Auf einer Höhe von bis zu 259 m bieten sich aus jedem der sechs Stockwerke spektakuläre Ausblicke über die gesamte Stadt. Der Bau befindet sich am Rockefeller Plaza, inmitten von 19 Gebäuden, die ein einmalig kunstvolles Ensemble des Art Deco bilden.

Au sommet de l'un des gratte-ciel les plus hauts du pays, cette terrasse d'observation a été récemment ré-ouverte dans un style inspiré des paquebots de croisière après une rénovation de 75 millions de dollars. Située à 260 m au-dessus du niveau de la rue au sommet du gratte-ciel de General Electric, la terrasse offre une vue spectaculaire sur la ville toute entière depuis chacun de ses six niveaux. Le gratte-ciel trône au sein du complexe des 19 bâtiments de Rockefeller Plaza, à l'exécution et au style Art Déco inégalés.

Situada sobre uno de los edificios más altos del país, esta terraza panorámica abrió recientemente sus puertas de nuevo con un diseño inspirado en los transatlánticos tras una renovación que ha costado 75 millones de dólares. Desde los 260 m de la azotea, la terraza del edificio de General Electric ofrece espectaculares vistas de la ciudad en cada una de sus seis alturas. El edificio se encuadra en un complejo de 19 torres en Rockefeller Plaza de un nivel artístico y estilo Art Déco incomparables.

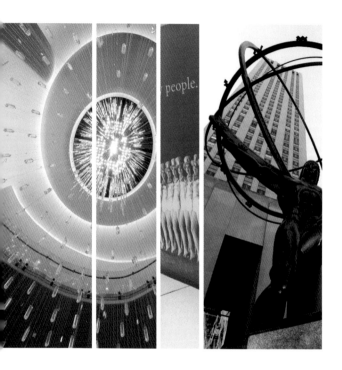

TOP OF THE ROCK

30 Rockefeller Plaza // Midtown
Tel.: +1 212 698 2000
www.topoftherocknyc.com

Mon–Sun 8 am to 12 pm
B, D, F, V to 47th-50th Sts Rockefeller Center
or E, V to 5th Ave 53rd St

Designed by Renzo Piano, winner of the honorable Pritzker, this 52-story glass skyscraper in Times Square is the third tallest building in New York with an impressive 1.5-million-sq-ft of space that provides its occupants with a sense of the city that surrounds them. The building boasts numerous innovations in environmentally sustainable design such as a combination of glass curtain wall and a scrim of ceramic tubes to reduce heat.

Dieser 52 Stockwerke hohe Glaswolkenkratzer am Times Square, entworfen von Pritzker-Preisträger Renzo Piano, ist das dritthöchste Gebäude in New York. Die beeindruckende Größe von 143 000 m² vermittelt jenen, die dort arbeiten, ein Gefühl für die Stadt, die sie umgibt. Das Gebäude bietet einige innovative umweltfreundliche Designlösungen, wie zum Beispiel die Verbindung von Glasvorhangfassaden und einem Netz aus Keramikröhren, welche die Sonneneinstrahlung reduziert.

Conçu par Renzo Piano, lauréat du prestigieux Pritzker Prize, ce gratte-ciel de verre de 52 étages à Times Square est la troisième plus haute tour de New York, avec une surface de près de 143 000 m² d'espace offrant à ses occupants une perception aigüe de la ville qui les entoure. Le bâtiment bénéficie de nombreuses innovations en matière de conception environnementale, telles que sa façade-rideau vitrée doublée d'un dispositif de brise-soleil en tubes de céramique.

Diseñado por Renzo Piano, ganador del prestigioso Pritzker Prize, el rascacielos acristalado de 52 plantas construido en Times Square es el tercer edificio más alto de Nueva York, y sus 143 000 m² transmiten a los ocupantes toda la sensación de la ciudad que les rodea. Al edificio se han incorporado numerosas innovaciones en diseño sostenible, como por ejemplo la combinación de muros vidriados y una pantalla de tubos cerámicos para reducir la absorción de calor.

NEW YORK TIMES BUILDING

620 8th Avenue // Midtown
www.newyorktimesbuilding.com

A, C, E, 1, 2, 3 to 42nd St Times Square

Considered one of the most recognizable structures in New York City, the Chrysler Building, designed by architect William Van Allen, is an iconic example of Art Deco architecture. Commissioned by the founder of the Chrysler Corporation, many of its architectural ornamentations were modeled after automobile products. Declared a national landmark in 1976, this Manhattan monument remains the world's tallest steel-supported brick structure and is renowned for its terraced crown and triangular vaulted windows.

Das Chrysler Building, entworfen von William Van Allen, gilt als eines der Gebäude mit dem höchsten Wiedererkennungswert in New York und ist eine Ikone der Art Deco-Architektur. Auftraggeber war der Gründer der Chrysler Corporation, aus diesem Grund sind viele dekorative Elemente Autoteilen nachempfunden. 1976 wurde das Gebäude unter Denkmalschutz gestellt. Das Chrysler Building ist weltweit der höchste stahlverstärkte Ziegelbau und ist berühmt für das abgestufte Dach mit seinen Dreiecksfenstern.

Considéré comme une icône New-Yorkaise, le Chrysler Building, conçu par l'architecte William Van Allen, est un exemple emblématique de l'architecture Art Déco. Il a été commandé par le fondateur de la Chrysler Corporation dont les produits automobiles ont inspiré la plupart de ses ornements architecturaux. Déclaré monument national en 1976, cette tour reste la plus grande construction en brique à charpente métallique du monde dont le couronnement en terrasses et les fenêtres triangulaires voûtées sont célèbres.

Considerada una de las estructuras más reconocibles de Nueva York, el edificio Chrysler, diseñado por el arquitecto William Van Allen, es un ejemplo paradigmático de arquitectura Art Déco. Encargado por el fundador de Chrysler Corporation, muchos de sus detalles se inspiran en piezas automovilísticas. Declarado monumento nacional en 1976, el edificio sigue siendo la estructura de ladrillo sobre acero más alta del mundo. A destacar la corona y las ventanas triangulares abovedadas.

CHRYSLER BUILDING

405 Lexington Avenue // Midtown
Tel.: +1 212 682 3070

7 to Grand Central Station
or 4, 5, 6, S to Grand Central 42nd St

GRAND CENTRAL STATION

87 East 42nd Street // Midtown
www.grandcentralterminal.com

Mon–Sun 5:30 am to 2 am
4, 5, 6, S to Grand Central 42nd St

A beautiful reminiscence of the golden era of long-distance passenger trains, this 49-acre "city within a city" is the largest train station in the world and houses over 100 retail stores and restaurants. With its elaborately decorated, vaulted astronomy-themed ceiling lit by 60-foot arched windows and Roman-inspired ramps, this Beaux Arts style landmark was extensively restored over a period of twelve years and is a timeless symbol of the continual motion present in the station's grand concourse that greets 750,000 people daily.

Ein schönes Relikt aus dem Goldenen Zeitalter der Eisenbahn. Diese „Stadt-in-der-Stadt" ist mit über 100 Geschäften und Restaurants und 20 ha Fläche der größte Bahnhof der Welt. Das Wahrzeichen des Beaux Art schmücken eine mit Sternzeichenmotiven verzierte gewölbte Decke, 18 m hohe Bogenfenster sowie römisch inspirierte Freitreppen. Der Bau wurde zwölf Jahre lang restauriert und ist ein zeitloses Symbol der ständigen Bewegung, die 750 000 Menschen hier täglich erleben.

Un souvenir magnifique de l'âge d'or des trains, cette « ville dans la ville » de près de 20 ha est la plus grande gare du monde et abrite plus de 100 boutiques et restaurants. Avec sa décoration élaborée, sa voûte en ciel astronomique éclairée par des fenêtres en arc de 18 m et des rampes d'inspiration romaine, cet édifice de style Beaux-Arts a subit une restauration qui a duré douze ans. C'est un symbole intemporel du mouvement perpétuel dans le grand hall de gare qui accueille 750 000 personnes par jour.

Hermosa reminiscencia de la edad de oro de los trenes de pasajeros de largo recorrido, la "ciudad dentro de una ciudad" es la mayor estación ferroviaria del mundo, y sus 200 000 m² albergan más de 100 tiendas y restaurantes. De techo abovedado y minuciosamente decorado e iluminado por ventanales de 19 m de alto, el complejo fue restaurado durante un periodo de doce años y es un símbolo intemporal del constante movimiento presente en la estación, que recibe diariamente a 750 000 personas.

This midtown Manhattan library is a cultural treasure chest of some of the world's greatest collections of rare books, musical and artistic works and illuminated manuscripts. The major renovation and expansion project spearheaded by architect Renzo Piano included doubling the exhibition space, adding an underground vault area with a 280-seat auditorium, and designing a modern steel-and-glass structure as its new Madison Avenue entrance.

Die Bibliothek ist eine Schatztruhe der Kulturen – hier befindet sich eine der größten Sammlungen seltener Bücher, musischer und künstlerischer Arbeiten und Manuskripte der Welt. Die großangelegte Renovierung und Vergrößerung wurde vom Architekten Renzo Piano geleitet. Hierbei wurde die Ausstellungsfläche verdoppelt, unterirdische Räumlichkeiten mit einem Auditorium mit 280 Sitzen sowie ein moderner Glas- und Stahlbau als neuer Eingang an der Madison Avenue geschaffen.

Cette bibliothèque est un trésor culturel contenant certaines des plus belles collections de livres rares, d'œuvres musicales et artistiques et de manuscrits enluminés au monde. Les importants travaux de rénovation et d'agrandissement dirigés par l'architecte Renzo Piano comprenaient le doublement de la surface d'exposition, l'ajout d'un sous-sol voûté avec un auditorium de 280 places, et la conception d'une structure moderne d'acier et de verre comme nouvelle entrée depuis Madison Avenue.

La librería es todo un tesoro cultural en el que encontrar algunas de las mejores colecciones de libros descatalogados, volúmenes musicales y artísticos y manuscritos iluminados de todo el mundo. El principal proyecto de renovación y expansión, iniciado por el arquitecto Renzo Piano, supuso doblar el espacio de exposición, así como la creación de un área abovedada subterránea con un auditorio para 280 personas y el diseño de una moderna estructura en vidrio y acero para su nueva entrada en Madison Avenue.

MORGAN LIBRARY EXPANSION

225 Madison Avenue // Midtown
www.themorgan.org

6 to 33rd St
or B, D, F, N, Q, R, V, W to 34th St Herald Square
or 4, 5, 6, S to Grand Central 42nd St

IAC HEADQUARTERS

555 West 18th Street // Chelsea
Tel.: +1 212 314 7300
www.iacbuilding.com

A, C, E, L to 8th Ave 14th St or A, E to 23rd St

Off the beaten path from the rigid structures of most office high-rise towers in New York, this building designed by architectural giant Frank Gehry is not only his first office building in Manhattan but also his first major glass building. The overall fluid form resembles tightly packed cells in a beehive that contort into two main levels even though it is actually a 10-story building.

Das erste Bürogebäude von Stararchitekt Frank Gehry in Manhattan ist auch sein erstes großes Gebäude aus Glas. Im Gegensatz zu den unzähligen strengen Strukturen anderer New Yorker Bürotürme zeichnet sich das IAC Headquarters durch seine durchgängig geschwungene Formgebung aus, die an eng aneinander liegende Bienenwaben erinnert. Das Gebäude ist in zwei vertikale Bereiche unterteilt, und umfasst insgesamt zehn Stockwerke.

Hors des sentiers battus de la rigidité structurelle de la plupart des tours de bureaux New-Yorkaises, ce bâtiment conçu par le géant de l'architecture, Frank Gehry, est non seulement son premier immeuble de bureaux à Manhattan, mais encore sa première construction de verre importante. La volumétrie fluide de l'ensemble ressemble aux rayons d'une ruche se courbant sur deux niveaux principaux, bien qu'il s'agisse en réalité d'une dizaine d'étages.

Punto y aparte con respecto a las rígidas estructuras de la mayoría de grandes torres de oficinas neoyorquinas, el edificio diseñado por el insigne Frank Gehry no sólo es su primer edificio de oficinas en Manhattan, sino también su primer gran edificio acristalado. La fluidez general de sus formas evoca las apretadas celdas de una colmena retorcida a dos alturas principales, pese a que en realidad el edificio tiene diez plantas.

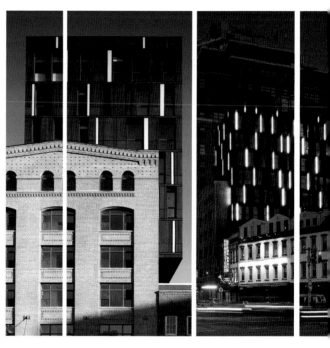

THE PORTER HOUSE

366 West 15th Street // Chelsea
Tel.: +1 212 755 5544

A, C, E, L to 8th Ave 14th St

Old architecture is celebrated at Porter House, the 22-unit luxury apartment development where a six-story old warehouse of yellow brick serves as the foundation for the newly designed addition. Four stories of zinc panels and glass rise above the original structure creating an interesting interplay between the old and the new. Designed by Gregg Pasquarelli of ShoP Architects, this building also uses a daring lighting system on its exterior, making it one of the most visually distinctive buildings in the city.

Das Porter House huldigt der alten Architektur: Bei dem luxuriösen Apartmenthaus mit 22 Wohnungen dient ein sechsstöckiges altes Lagerhaus aus gelben Ziegeln als Fundament für den neu entworfenen Aufbau. Über dem ursprünglichen Baukörper erheben sich vier Stockwerke aus Zinkplatten und Glas und schaffen ein interessantes Zusammenspiel von Alt und Neu. An dem Bau inszenierte Gregg Pasquarelli von ShoP Architects eine extravagante Fassadenbeleuchtung und schuf so eines der optisch markantesten Gebäude der Stadt.

La Porter House célèbre l'ancienne architecture. Dans ce développement de 22 appartements de luxe, un vieil entrepôt de six étages en brique jaune sert de base à la nouvelle extension. Quatre étages de verre et de zinc s'élèvent au-dessus de la structure originelle et créent une interaction intéressante entre l'ancien et le moderne. Conçu par Gregg Pasquarelli de ShoP Architects, ce bâtiment utilise aussi un système d'éclairage audacieux à l'extérieur, qui en fait l'un des bâtiments les plus visuellement distinctifs de la ville.

Porter House es un triunfo de la arquitectura tradicional: las seis plantas de ladrillo amarillo de un antiguo almacén prestan las bases para un nuevo proyecto de 22 apartamentos de lujo. Cuatro plantas de paneles de zinc y vidrio se alzan sobre la estructura original, creando una curiosa interrelación entre lo viejo y lo nuevo. Diseñado por Gregg Pasquarelli, de ShoP Architects, el edificio utiliza en el exterior un atrevido sistema de luces que hace de él uno de los más fácilmente identificables de la ciudad.

A

THE HIGH LINE

After more than two years of construction and with over 200 species of plants, this elevated railroad track has been revived into a beautiful contemporary garden designed by architectural firm Diller Scofidio + Renfro and landscape architecture firm James Corner Field Operations. Using the abandoned tracks as a guide for the planting beds, the High Line embraces its rough, industrial roots. By keeping the main infrastructure in place, the landscape is a subtle dance between the cultivated and tranquil beauty of modern design and urban decay.

Mehr als zwei Jahre Bauzeit und über 200 Pflanzenarten ließen diese Hochbahngleise als eleganten modernen Garten wiederauferstehen. Der Entwurf stammt vom Architekturbüro Diller Scofidio + Renfro und dem Landschaftsarchitekturbüro James Corner Field Operations. Entlang der verlassenen Gleise wurden Pflanzenbeete angelegt und so die raue, industrielle Herkunft der Hochbahn einbezogen. Der Park wirkt dadurch wie ein feinsinniges Zusammenspiel von kultivierter, ruhiger Schönheit modernen Designs und urbanem Verfall.

Après plus de deux ans de chantier et grâce à plus de 200 espèces de plantes, cette voie ferrée aérienne a été réhabilitée en un splendide jardin contemporain imaginé par les architectes de Diller Scofidio + Renfro et les paysagistes de James Corner Operations. En utilisant la voie ferrée abandonnée pour guider les jardinières, la High Line exprime ses racines industrielles brutes. L'infrastructure principale a été conservée pour faire du paysage une danse subtile entre la beauté tranquille et cultivée de la modernité et le déclin urbain.

Tras más de dos años de construcción, la antigua vía férrea elevada se ha reencarnado en un hermoso jardín contemporáneo con más de 200 tipos de plantas, diseñado por los arquitectos Diller Scofidio + Renfro y la empresa paisajista James Corner Field Operations. Al aprovechar las vías como lecho para las plantas, el High Line proclama orgulloso sus raíces industriales. El complejo mantiene intacta la estructura principal y alcanza así un delicado equilibrio entre la belleza serena y cultivada del diseño moderno y el declive urbano.

THE HIGH LINE

Gansevoort Street to 34th Street between
10th and 11th Avenues // Meatpacking District, Chelsea
Tel.: +1 212 500 6035
www.thehighline.org

Mon–Sun 7 am to 10 pm
A, C, E, L to 8th Ave 14th St

Sitting atop 56-ft concrete support columns, The Standard by Polshek Partnership Architects rises above the Meatpacking District and straddles the Highline, integrating the park into its architecture. Named the Municipal Art Society's Best New Building of 2009, the 20-story hotel draws on a century of modern architecture with its solid lines, hard surfaces and cubist aesthetic. The floor-to-ceiling windows bring the city inside while also hinting at the voyeuristic interplay between hotel patrons and visitors to the park below.

Auf 17 m hohen Säulen ragt das Hotel von Polshek Partnership Architects über den Meatpacking District, überspannt die High Line und bezieht den Park in den Bau ein. Die Formensprache des zwanzigstöckigen Hotels, ausgezeichnet mit dem Municipal Art Society Preis für das beste neue Gebäude 2009, zitiert ein Jahrhundert moderner Architekturgeschichte: klare Linien, harte Oberflächen und kubistische Ästhetik. Raumhohe Fenster laden die Stadt ins Innere ein und erlauben ein voyeuristisches Wechselspiel von Hotelgästen und Parkbesuchern.

Perché sur des jambes de béton de 17 m, l'hôtel de 20 étages de Polshek Partnership Architects chevauche la High Line, l'intégrant à son architecture. Nommé meilleur nouvel édifice en 2009 par la Municipal Art Society, ses lignes droites, ses surfaces dures et son esthétique cubiste se fondent sur un siècle d'architecture moderne. Le vitrage toute hauteur amène la ville à l'intérieur tout en suggérant une interaction visuelle entre les clients de l'hôtel et les visiteurs du parc en contrebas.

Asentado sobre pilares de hormigón de 17 m de alto, The Standard, obra de Polshek Partnership Architects, se eleva a horcajadas sobre el High Line, integrando el parque en la arquitectura. Designado Mejor Edificio Nuevo por la Municipal Art Society en 2009, el hotel recupera un siglo de arquitectura moderna en sus líneas sólidas, duras superficies y estética cubista. Los inmensos ventanales invitan la ciudad al interior y apuntan a la interacción voyeurística entre huéspedes del hotel y visitantes del parque.

THE CENTER FOR ARCHITECTURE

536 LaGuardia Place // Greenwich Village
Tel.: +1 212 683 0023
www.aiany.org

Mon–Fri 9 am to 8 pm, Sat 11 am to 5 pm
A, B, C, D, E, F, V to W 4th St or 6 to Bleecker St

Considered the city's leading cultural institution focused on architecture, the center hosts a diverse lineup of exhibitions concentrated on the built environment and offers design resources, educational programs and tours for the profession and the public alike. Its incredible 15,000-sq-ft space, designed by Andrew Berman in 2003, has three floors of high ceilings filled with natural light, and includes one of the first geothermal systems in New York.

Das Center gilt als führende Einrichtung für Architektur in New York. Das Angebot umfasst unterschiedlichste Ausstellungen – Schwerpunkt ist das Thema bebaute Umwelt. Ebenso gehören Design als Inspirationsquelle, Bildungsangebote und Führungen für Profis oder Amateure zum Programm. Im Jahr 2003 konzipierte Andrew Berman diese beeindruckende, 1 400m² große Fläche: Tageslicht durchflutet drei Stockwerke, jeweils mit hohen Decken und außerdem wurde eines der ersten Erdwärmesysteme in New York eingebaut.

Considéré comme l'institution culturelle phare de la ville pour l'architecture, le centre accueille une programmation diversifiée d'expositions concentrées sur l'environnement bâti et propose des ressources de conception, des programmes éducatifs et des visites pour les professionnels aussi bien que le public. Son espace incroyable de 1 400 m², conçu par Andrew Berman en 2003, comporte trois hauts étages baignés de lumière naturelle, et comprend l'un des premiers systèmes géothermiques de New York.

Considerado la principal institución cultural de la ciudad en cuestiones arquitectónicas, el centro acoge toda una serie de exposiciones centradas en entornos edificados y ofrece recursos de diseño, programas educativos y visitas guiadas para profesionales y aficionados. Sus 1 400 m² de superficie, diseñados por Andrew Berman en 2003, se extienden a lo largo de tres luminosas plantas de altos techos e incluyen uno de los primeros sistemas geotérmicos de Nueva York.

A

The 175,000-sq-ft New Academic Building of the Cooper Union School is as technologically advanced and innovative as the free and accessible education in art, architecture and engineering the 150-year-old institution is known for. This soaring nine-story futuristic structure, designed by Thom Mayne of Morphosis with Gruzen Samton, has unexpected architectural elements such as a Grand Atrium the full height of the building. It is also the first LEED-certified academic laboratory building in New York.

Das 16 200 m² große Akademiegebäude der 150 Jahre alten Cooper Union School ist ebenso technisch fortschrittlich und innovativ, wie es dem Ruf der frei zugänglichen Schule für Kunst, Architektur und Ingenieurswesen entspricht. Der neunstöckige, hoch aufragende futuristische Bau, entworfen von Thom Mayne (Morphosis) mit Gruzen Samton, weist unerwartete Architekturelemente auf, wie zum Beispiel das große Atrium, das sich über die Gesamthöhe des Hauses erstreckt.

Les 16 200 m² du nouveau bâtiment académique de la Cooper Union School sont aussi technologiquement avancés et innovant que l'enseignement gratuit et accessible de l'art, de l'architecture et de l'ingénierie pour lequel cette institution vieille de 150 ans est connue. Cette structure futuriste élevée de neuf étages, conçue par Thom Mayne de Morphosis en partenariat avec Gruzen Samton, comporte des éléments architecturaux inattendus tel son grand atrium couvrant toute la hauteur du bâtiment.

El nuevo edificio académico de Cooper Union School destaca tanto por los avances e innovaciones tecnológicas que albergan sus 16 200 m² como por la accesible y gratuita formación en arte, arquitectura e ingeniería por la que es conocida la institución de 150 años. La futurista estructura de nueve plantas, diseñada por Thom Mayne, de Morphosis, junto con Gruzen Samton, cuenta con elementos arquitectónicos inesperados, como un gran atrio abierto hasta el techo.

COOPER UNION SCHOOL OF ART

41 Cooper Square // Bowery
Tel.: +1 212 353 4100
www.cooper.edu/art

Tours given every Tue at 12:30 pm
with the exception of holidays
6 to Astor Place or R, W to 8th St NYU

COOPER SQUARE HOTEL

Set amid the 19th-century tenement buildings of the East Village, the Cooper Square Hotel's 21-story glass and steel edifice defines the relationship between old and new architecture in New York. It is progressive and modern in design, yet recognizes its place among a traditional neighborhood. Architect Carlos Zapata imagined the building as a face, small at the neck and widening upwards, as a way to give it a distinct personality and create a dynamic, sculptural form that has been described as a glass wing over the Bowery.

Das 21 Stockwerke hohe Cooper Square Hotel, ein Gebäude aus Glas und Stahl, liegt inmitten der Wohnhäuser des 19. Jahrhunderts im East Village und vermittelt zwischen alter und neuer Architektur in New York. Der Bau ist progressiv und modern, trägt aber seiner traditionellen Umgebung Rechnung. Architekt Carlos Zapata ließ sich bei seinem Entwurf von der Form des Gesichts inspirieren: ein schmaler Hals und nach oben hin breiter werdend. Das verleiht dem Gebäude den eigenen Charakter und schafft eine dynamische, skulpturale Form – ein Glasflügel über der Bowery.

Situé au cœur des logements du XIXe siècle de l'East Village, les 21 étages de verre et d'acier de cet hôtel sont l'essence de la relation entre l'ancien et le moderne à New York. L'architecte Carlos Zapata l'a imaginé comme un visage, petit à la nuque et s'élargissant par le haut, afin de lui donner une physionomie distincte et de créer une forme dynamique et sculpturale qui a été décrite comme une aile de verre sur le Bowery.

Ubicado entre los decimonónicos edificios de viviendas del East Village, el Cooper Square Hotel define la relación entre la arquitectura antigua y moderna en Nueva York. El arquitecto Carlos Zapata imaginó el edificio de 21 plantas como un rostro de cuello estrecho que se ensancha a medida que asciende para darle una personalidad individual y crear una forma dinámica y escultural, que algunos describen como un ala de cristal sobre el Bowery.

COOPER SQUARE HOTEL

25 Cooper Square // Bowery
Tel.: +1 212 475 5700
www.thecoopersquarehotel.com

6 to Astor Place or R, W to 8th St NYU

A

40 BOND

40 BOND

40 Bond Street // East Village
www.40bond.com

6 to Bleecker St
or B, D, F, V to Broadway-Lafayette St

Swiss architects Herzog & de Meuron's luxury condo, which was awarded a 2009 Professional Design Award, puts an avant-guard spin on the idea of downtown lofts. Taking into account the cast iron buildings so common in NoHo, 40 Bond has reinvented the traditional look with a combination of poured concrete, a glass facade wrapped in a grid of curved, green glass and a graffiti-inspired cast aluminum gate—New York's answer to the picket fence.

Der Luxuswohnkomplex, gebaut von den Schweizer Architekten Herzog & de Meuron, verleiht dem Typus des innenstädtischen Lofts avantgardistische Züge. Die für NoHo typischen gusseisernen Elemente aufnehmend, schafft 40 Bond eine neue Architektursprache durch den Einsatz von Gussbeton, einer Glasfassade, überspannt von einem gebogenen grünlichen Glasgitter, und einem von Graffitiformen inspiriertem Tor aus Gussaluminium – die New Yorker Antwort auf den Lattenzaun.

Ces appartements de luxe conçus par les architectes suisses Herzog & de Meuron constituent une interprétation avant-gardiste du loft en centre-ville. S'inspirant des bâtiments traditionnels en fonte de NoHo, 40 Bond réinvente leur aspect en combinant le béton coulé à une façade de verre enveloppée dans un calepinage de verre courbe vert et une grille d'aluminium inspirée des graffiti – l'interprétation New Yorkaise de la palissade.

Los apartamentos concebidos por los arquitectos suizos Herzog & de Meuron dan una vuelta de tuerca vanguardista al concepto de los lofts en el centro de la ciudad. Respetando los edificios de hierro fundido propios de NoHo, 40 Bond reinventa su apariencia tradicional con el uso del cemento, una fachada acristalada enmarcada en una malla de cristal verde y curvo y una puerta de aluminio inspirada en el grafitti, la respuesta neoyorquina a la tradicional verja de madera.

Considered more like a work of sculpture one lives in, this unique 16-story building is the first residential project of the internationally acclaimed architect Bernard Tschumi. This 32-unit high-end condominium building has luxurious design elements not usually found in the edgy Lower East Side, such as floor-to-ceiling windows and private terraces, and is the first 24-hour doorman apartment building in the neighborhood.

Dieses einzigartige 16-stöckige Gebäude wirkt fast wie eine Skulptur, die bewohnt werden kann. Es ist das erste Wohnprojekt des international bekannten Architekten Bernard Tschumi. Das Gebäude umfasst 32 Wohneinheiten der Extraklasse und bietet luxuriöse Designelemente, die es so in der Lower East Side selten gibt, wie zum Beispiel raumhohe Fenster und Privatterrassen. Außerdem ist es das erste Gebäude im Viertel, das rund um die Uhr einen Portierdienst anbietet.

Volontiers considéré comme une oeuvre de sculpture dans laquelle on vit, ce bâtiment unique de 16 étages est le premier projet résidentiel de Bernard Tschumi, un architecte à la renommée internationale. Cette unité de 32 appartements haut-de-gamme contient des éléments de luxe que l'on ne trouve habituellement pas dans le style de la Lower East Side, telles que les fenêtres toute hauteur et les terrasses privées. C'est aussi la première résidence du quartier avec un portier permanent.

Hay quien considera el primer proyecto residencial del respetado arquitecto Bernard Tschumi no tanto un edificio singular de 16 plantas como una escultura habitable. Las 32 unidades de alto standing del edificio cuentan con detalles de lujo no habituales en el poco convencional Lower East Side, como grandes ventanales y terrazas privadas. Es también el primer edificio de apartamentos del barrio con servicio de conserje las 24 horas del día.

BLUE CONDOMINIUM

105 Norfolk Avenue // Lower East Side
Tel.: +1 212 533 8822
www.bluecondonyc.com

F, J, M, Z to Essex St / Delancey

40 MERCER RESIDENCES

40 Mercer Street // SoHo
www.40mercersoho.com

N, Q, R, W to Canal St or A, C, E to Canal St

Developer André Balazs commissioned famed architect Jean Nouvel to customize a one-of-a-kind modern apartment building in the distinctively historical cast-iron neighborhood of SoHo. The first residential project in Manhattan for neo-modernist Nouvel, this 13-story building houses 41 uniquely styled apartments designed like artist's lofts with all rooms adjoining each other in the traditional French way.

Der Bauherr André Balazs beauftragte den berühmten Architekten Jean Nouvel mit dem Entwurf eines einzigartigen modernen Apartmenthauses in dem unverwechselbaren, von gusseisernen Konstruktionen geprägten Viertel von SoHo. Für Nouvel, einem Vertreter der Neo-Moderne, war dies das erste Wohnprojekt in Manhattan. Das 13-stöckige Gebäude beheimatet 41 individuell gestaltete Apartments, die wie Künstlerlofts angelegt sind, in denen man nach französischer Art von einem Raum zum anderen gelangt.

Cette commande du promoteur André Balazs au célèbre architecte Jean Nouvel exigeait un immeuble d'habitation moderne unique en son genre dans le quartier historique de SoHo où l'architecture en fonte est si distincte. Premier projet résidentiel à Manhattan pour cet architecte néo-moderniste, ce bâtiment de 13 étages abrite 41 appartements au style exceptionnel, conçus comme des lofts d'artistes où l'espace est agencé en une suite de pièces à la manière traditionnelle française.

El promotor André Balazs encargó al conocido arquitecto Jean Nouvel que personalizase un moderno y singular edificio de apartamentos en SoHo, un barrio tradicionalmente conocido por sus estructuras de hierro fundido. Primer proyecto residencial del neomodernista Nouvel en Manhattan, las 13 plantas del edificio albergan 41 apartamentos con carácter individual, concebidos como lofts de artista en los que todas las habitaciones conectan entre sí, al estilo francés.

A

NATIONAL SEPTEMBER 11
MEMORIAL AND MUSEUM

World Trade Center // Downtown
www.national911memorial.org

E to World Trade Center Station

Designed by architect Michael Arad and landscape architect Peter Walker, the Memorial honors the nearly 3,000 victims of the terrorist attacks of both 1993 and 2001 by creating a meditative space of nearly 400 trees in clustered formation broken up by two large recessed pools. Set within the footprints of the Twin Towers, the eight-acre Memorial Plaza serves to remember the lives lost by inscribing their names alongside the largest manmade waterfalls in the country.

Das Mahnmal, entworfen von Architekt Michael Arad und Landschaftsarchitekt Peter Walker, erinnert an die fast 3 000 Opfer der Terroranschläge von 1993 und 2001. Es entsteht eine meditative Anlage mit 400 Bäumen, die zwei große Bassins umgeben. Das Denkmal wird in den „Fußabdrücken" der früheren Twin Towers gebaut. Ein drei ha großes Areal, die Memorial Plaza, soll die Erinnerung an alle, die ihr Leben verloren, wach halten. Ihre Namen werden entlang der größten künstlichen Wasserfälle des Landes zu lesen sein.

Conçu par l'architecte Michael Arad et le paysagiste Peter Walker, le Mémorial perpétue le souvenir de près de 3 000 victimes des attentats terroristes de 1993 et de 2001 en créant un espace de méditation formé de deux grands bassins encaissés et disposés au milieu d'une place boisée de 400 arbres. Installés sur l'empreinte des tours jumelles, les trois ha du Mémorial honorent la mémoire de ceux qui y ont perdu la vie en inscrivant leurs noms à côté des plus grandes chutes d'eau artificielles du pays.

Diseñado por el arquitecto Michael Arad y el paisajista Peter Walker, el Memorial honra el recuerdo de las casi 3 000 víctimas de los ataques terroristas de 1993 y 2001 y ofrece un espacio para la reflexión marcado por casi 400 árboles plantados en torno de dos grandes piscinas en cascada. Delimitada por el plano original de las Torres Gemelas, las más de tres ha de Memorial Plaza conservan el recuerdo de las vidas perdidas: sus nombres aparecen inscritos junto a las mayores cascadas artificiales del país.

DAVID CHILDS

As the Consulting Design Partner of Skidmore, Owings and Merrill, David Childs has been responsible for many of the landmark buildings in the New York City skyline. He has received the Medal of Honor by the New York chapter of the American Institute of Architects in 2010 for his body of work, ranging from the newly constructed Time Warner Center to the preservation of the Lever House, yet he earned his worldwide reputation for his work on Ground Zero. With the awe-inspiring structure of Seven World Trade Center recently completed, Childs is now heading what will be one of New York's most iconic projects, the main building of the World Trade Center formerly named Freedom Tower. Devised as the strongest building in the world with a concrete core and steel frame, its sky-high frame will dominate the downtown skyline.

In seiner Funktion als Consultant Design Partner bei Skidmore, Owings and Merrill (SOM) ist David Childs für einige charakteristische Wolkenkratzer in New York verantwortlich. Im Jahr 2010 wurde er für seine Arbeit mit der Ehrenmedaille der New Yorker Sektion der amerikanischen Architektenvereinigung ausgezeichnet. Weltweit bekannt wurde sein Werk, das den Neubau des Time Warner Center und die Restaurierung des Lever House einschließt, durch seine Arbeit am Ground Zero. Nach der Fertigstellung des eindrucksvollen Seven World Trade Center leitet Childs nun den Bau des zentralen Gebäudes des World Trade Center, ehemals als Freedom Tower bekannt, eines der prestigeträchtigsten Projekte New Yorks. Der Betonkern und die Stahlrahmenkonstruktion werden dieses Gebäude zum stabilsten der Welt machen, dessen Gestalt künftig die Skyline von Downtown Manhattan bestimmen wird.

En tant que consultant de conception associé de Skidmore, Owings & Merrill (SOM), David Childs a signé de nombreux bâtiments phares du décor new-yorkais. Bien qu'il ait reçu la Médaille d'Honneur de la section new-yorkaise de l'American Institute of Architects en 2010 pour l'ensemble de son travail, du récent Time Warner Center à la restauration de la Lever House, sa réputation mondiale est dûe au projet du Ground Zero sur le site des tours jumelles. Depuis l'achèvement récent de la structure imposante du Seven World Trade Center, Childs dirige ce qui sera un projet emblématique de New York, la tour principale du World Trade Center auparavant nommée Freedom Tower. Conçue comme la construction la plus solide du monde avec un noyau en béton et une charpente en acier, sa structure de hauteur céleste dominera les tours de Downtown Manhattan.

En tanto que socio y asesor de diseño de Skidmore, Owings and Merrill(SOM), David Childs es responsable de muchos de los edificios emblemáticos de la silueta de Nueva York. Ha merecido la medalla de honor de la delegación neoyorquina del American Institute of Architects en 2010 por el conjunto de su obra, que va desde el recientemente construido Time Warner Center hasta la conservación de Lever House; con todo, debe su fama internacional a su trabajo en el Ground Zero. La imponente estructura del Seven World Trade Center está ya completada, con ella, Childs ha puesto en marcha el que será uno de los proyectos más definitorios de Nueva York, el edificio principal del World Trade Center, anteriormente llamado Freedom Tower. Diseñado como el edificio más resistente del mundo, con núcleo de acero y estructura de acero, su inmensa silueta marcará la imagen de la ciudad.

SKYSCRAPER MUSEUM

39 Battery Place // Battery Park
Tel.: +1 212 968 1961
www.skyscraper.org

Wed–Sun 12 pm to 6 pm
R, W to Bowling Green Station

With stainless steel floors and spaciously designed interiors, this one room museum focuses on the construction, history and social importance of high-rise buildings as objects of design and products of today's most impressive technological advances. As the home of all things skyscraper, it is only appropriate that SOM, the famed architectural firm that pioneered the modern skyscraper, designed the museum. The original model and history of the World Trade Center are also on display as a special tribute to 9/11.

Das Museum, ein einziger Raum mit Edelstahlböden und großzügiger Innenaufteilung, befasst sich mit Bauweise, Geschichte und gesellschaftlicher Bedeutung des Hochhauses als Designobjekt und als Ergebnis technologischer Fortschritte. Hier findet man alles über Wolkenkratzer, und so war es logisch, dass das berühmte Büro SOM, Meister der Hochhausarchitektur, das Museum konzipierte. Das Originalmodell des World Trade Centers und dessen Geschichte werden zur Erinnerung an den 11. September ausgestellt.

Avec ses sols en acier inox et son intérieur spacieux, cette salle est consacrée à la construction, l'histoire et l'importance sociale des gratte-ciel comme objets de conception et produits des avancées technologiques actuelles les plus impressionnantes. Comme il abrite tout ce qui touche aux gratte-ciel, ce musée se devait d'être conçu par SOM, le célèbre cabinet d'architecture qui a ouvert la voie des tours modernes. La maquette originale et l'histoire du World Trade Center y sont présentées en souvenir des événements du 11 Septembre 2001.

De suelos de acero inoxidable y espaciosos interiores, el museo se concentra en la construcción, la historia y la importancia social de los rascacielos como objetos de diseño y productos de los más impresionantes avances tecnológicos de la actualidad. En tanto que instancia superior en la materia, resulta apropiado que SOM, la empresa pionera en la construcción moderna de rascacielos, diseñase el museo. El modelo original y la historia del World Trade Center se exponen aquí en recuerdo de lo sucedido el 11-S.

DESIGN

D

As the epicenter for design and fashion, New York City is not only a place of big concepts, but daring ones. It is a city that recognizes, promotes and celebrates those who are willing to experiment with the impossible, and serves as the world stage for the power of design. New York is the perfect fertile environment where adventurous designers from all over the world can incubate and launch their new design concepts, in turn bringing a great deal of diversity to the mix. Whether it be edgy downtown shops celebrating the casual styles of bohemian culture or the newest hotel designs taking on a contemporary approach to carefully curated chaos and old-school vintage, the ever-changing design styles of New York urban living is constantly reinvented and reborn, all the while setting the trends for the other parts of the world. But even with all the continual changes, the spirit of design in New York always stays the same: fresh, bold and striving to be best in the world.

New York ist das Zentrum für Mode und Design – hier gibt es keinesfalls nur große Ideen und Konzepte, sondern vor allem auch sehr gewagte. Die Stadt erkennt, fördert und feiert all jene, die sich auf einen Versuch mit dem Unmöglichen einlassen. Um die Macht des Designs zu erleben, blickt die Welt nach New York. Die Stadt bietet ein sehr anregendes Umfeld für abenteuerlustige Designer aus der ganzen Welt, die hier ihre neuen Designkonzepte entwickeln und vorstellen können, was wiederum zur Kulturvielfalt beiträgt. Ob ausgefallene Geschäfte, in denen ein entspannter Bohemien-Stil zelebriert wird, oder neuste Hotelentwürfe, bei denen zeitgenössische Gestaltung mit sorgfältig orchestriertem Chaos und ausgesuchten Vintage-Stücken in Einklang gebracht werden – die wechselnden Designrichtungen des urbanen New Yorker Lebens werden ständig weiterentwickelt und neu erfunden und setzen somit Trends für den Rest der Welt. Trotz dieses ständigen Wandels, bleibt das Design in New York sich selbst treu: frisch, gewagt und immer darauf bedacht, Weltklasse zu sein.

En tant qu'épicentre de la conception et de la mode, New York ne se contente pas de grands concepts. Ceux-ci doivent être audacieux. Elle reconnaît, encourage et récompense ceux qui osent expérimenter l'impossible, et sert de scène mondiale à la puissance du design. New York est le substrat fertile idéal où les concepteurs aventureux du monde entier peuvent couver et lancer leurs nouveaux concepts, qui à leur tour apportent une grande diversité à la composition. Que ce soit les magasins tendance du downtown qui célèbrent le style bohème, ou le design dernier cri des hôtels et son approche contemporaine du chaos soigneusement organisé ou du old-school authentique, les styles toujours changeant de la vie urbaine new-yorkaise renaissent et se réinventent constamment, tout en fixant la tendance pour le reste du monde. Mais même à travers ce changement perpétuel, l'esprit de la conception reste le même à New York : frais, audacieux et s'efforçant d'être le meilleur du monde.

Como epicentro del diseño y la moda, Nueva York no es sólo un lugar de grandes conceptos, sino de los más atrevidos. Es una ciudad que reconoce, promueve y celebra a aquellos que quieren experimentar con lo imposible y actúa como escena mundial para el poder del diseño. Nueva York es el ambiente fértil perfecto donde los diseñadores más aventureros de todo el mundo pueden incubar y lanzar sus nuevas ideas, aportando a su vez una gran diversidad a la mezcla. Ya se trate de las inquietas tiendas del centro, celebrando los estilos casuales de la cultura bohemia, o de los últimos diseños de hoteles adoptando un acercamiento contemporáneo al caos cuidadosamente organizado y al vintage de la vieja escuela, los siempre cambiantes estilos de la vida urbana de Nueva York se reinventan y renacen, marcando siempre las tendencias en todo el mundo. Pero a pesar de los continuos cambios, el espíritu diseñador de Nueva York es siempre el mismo: fresco, atrevido y esforzándose por ser el mejor del mundo.

ROOM MATE GRACE

125 West 45th Street // Midtown
Tel.: +1 212 354 2323
www.room-matehotels.com

B, D, F, V to 47th-50th Sts Rockefeller Center Station or
1,2,3, 7, N, Q, R, S, W to Times Square 42nd St Station

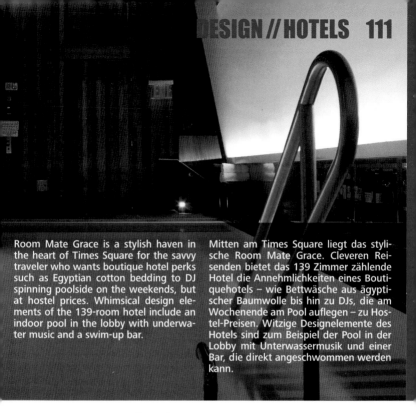

Room Mate Grace is a stylish haven in the heart of Times Square for the savvy traveler who wants boutique hotel perks such as Egyptian cotton bedding to DJ spinning poolside on the weekends, but at hostel prices. Whimsical design elements of the 139-room hotel include an indoor pool in the lobby with underwater music and a swim-up bar.

Mitten am Times Square liegt das stylische Room Mate Grace. Cleveren Reisenden bietet das 139 Zimmer zählende Hotel die Annehmlichkeiten eines Boutiquehotels – wie Bettwäsche aus ägyptischer Baumwolle bis hin zu DJs, die am Wochenende am Pool auflegen – zu Hostel-Preisen. Witzige Designelemente des Hotels sind zum Beispiel der Pool in der Lobby mit Unterwassermusik und einer Bar, die direkt angeschwommen werden kann.

Le Room Mate Grace est un havre de paix élégant au cœur de Times Square pour le voyageur futé qui veut les avantages d'un hôtel-boutique, de la literie en coton égyptien aux weekends piscine avec DJ, mais au prix d'une auberge. Les éléments de conception saugrenus de cet hôtel de 139 chambres incluent une piscine dans le hall d'accueil avec musique subaquatique et bar accessible à la nage.

Room Mate Grace es un elegante refugio en pleno Times Square para el avezado viajero que busca detallitos especiales en el servicio del hotel, como ropa de cama de algodón egipcio o un DJ junto a la piscina los fines de semana, todo ello a precios de pensión. Entre los caprichosos elementos de diseño de este hotel de 139 habitaciones cabe destacar la piscina interior en el recibidor con música submarina y un bar a ras de agua.

The 260 rooms in this intimate hotel are decorated in an old-school style with graffiti artwork, authentic vintage pieces and exposed concrete walls and plumbing pipes. The large communal living room in the lobby caters to the hipster set as DJs play music. The adjoining restaurant, The Breslin, is a modern twist of the British gastropub, and Stumptown Coffee Roasters emphasizes a no-gimmicks approach to décor with its standing-only espresso bar.

Die 260 Zimmer in diesem intimen Hotel sind im Old-School-Stil gestaltet: Graffitikunst, echte Vintage-Stücke, unverkleidete Betonwände und Rohrleitungen. Die Lobby dient als gemeinschaftliches Wohnzimmer und Szenetreff, in dem DJs auflegen. Das angeschlossene Restaurant, The Breslin, ist die moderne Version des britischen Gastropubs, und im Stumptown Coffee Roasters wird das schnörkellose Designkonzept mit einer Espresso-Stehbar noch betont.

ACE HOTEL

Les 260 chambres de cet hôtel accueillant sont décorées dans un style old-school incluant graffiti, pièces de collection authentiques, murs en béton apparent et tuyaux de plomberie. Le grand salon du hall répond à tous les besoins de sa clientèle bobo pendant que des DJs assurent. Le restaurant attenant, The Breslin, est une version moderne du gastropub britannique et la décoration du Stumptown Coffee Roasters va à l'essentiel, où l'on ne peut prendre son expresso que debout au comptoir.

Las 260 habitaciones de este int hotel están decoradas al estilo ar con graffitis, auténticas piezas vint paredes de hormigón visto y fonta descubierta. Un DJ pincha en el es so salón común del vestíbulo y ref el carácter in del establecimiento. taurante contiguo The Breslin ofre reinterpretación de la gastronom los pubs británicos, mientras que fetería sin mesas de Stumptown C Roasters incide en el enfoque espa de la decoración.

ACE HOTEL

20 West 29th Street // Midtown
Tel.: +1 212 679 2222
www.acehotel.com/newyork

R, W to 28th St Station

STUMPTOWN COFFEE ROASTERS

18 West 29th Street // Midtown
Tel.: +1 212 679 2222
www.stumptowncoffee.com

Mon–Sun 6 am to 8 pm

THE BRESLIN BAR & DINING ROOM

16 West 29th Street // Midtown
Tel.: +1 212 679 1939
www.thebreslin.com

Mon–Fri 7 am to 11.45 am (breakfast),
noon to 4 pm (lunch), 5.30 pm to midnight
(dinner), Sat–Sun 7 am to 4 pm (brunch),
5.30 to 12 pm (dinner)

Following the renovation and redesign of the Gramercy Park Hotel, hotelier Ian Schrager brought modern glamour back to the once-famous 1920s era hotel: the fabrics are thick and lush, the furniture is oversized and mysterious, the tile is a Moroccan import, and the decorative accents are bold and unique. Adding to this eclectic aesthetic are the Rose and Jade bars that double as galleries for paintings by the likes of Warhol and Basquiat.

Mit der Renovierung und dem neuen Design des Gramercy Park Hotels ist es Hotelier Ian Schrager gelungen, modernen Glanz in das einst berühmte 20er Jahre Hotel zurückzubringen: Die Stoffe sind üppig, das Mobiliar ist übergroß und geheimnisvoll, die Kacheln kommen aus Marokko und die dekorativen Akzente sind einzigartig und kühn. Die abwechslungsreiche Ästhetik wird von der Rose Bar und der Jade Bar noch verstärkt – sie sind Bar und Galerie zugleich, gezeigt werden Bilder von Künstlern wie Warhol und Basquiat.

Suite à la rénovation et la restructuration du Gramercy Park Hotel, le directeur Ian Schrager a ravivé le glamour moderne autrefois célèbre des années 1920: les tissus sont épais et luxuriants, les meubles sont surdimensionnés et mystérieux, les carrelages sont d'importation marocaine, et la décoration est audacieuse et originale. S'ajoutant à cette esthétique éclectique, les bars Rose et Jade servent aussi de galeries pour des œuvres d'artistes tels que Warhol et Basquiat.

Tras la renovación y remodelación del Gramercy Park Hotel, el hotelero Ian Schrager devolvió el glamour a un hotel famoso en la década de 1920: las telas son gruesas y suntuosas, el mobiliario enorme y misterioso; los azulejos marroquíes, de importación; y todos los detalles decorativos atrevidos y únicos. Los bares Rose y Jade, escenario también de exposiciones de Warhol, Basquiat y artistas de similar calibre, completan el eclecticismo del establecimiento.

GRAMERCY PARK HOTEL

2 Lexington Avenue // Gramercy Park
Tel.: +1 212 920 3300
www.gramercyparkhotel.com

6 to 23rd St Station

IAN
SCHRAG

Famed visionary in the world of the fashionable life, Ian Schrager has modernized the way we travel with his ground-breaking concepts in the hospitality industry. He first started his career with his late business partner Steve Rubell in the 1970s with the legendary Studio 54 before developing the first design hotel in the mid-80s with the "urban resort" concept where the guests in the public areas are the starring attraction. Schrager went on to complete seven more hotels, in turn creating the template for the ubiquitous boutique hotel. By collaborating with artists such as Julian Schnabel and Philippe Starck to create one-of-a-kind designs and cultivating a unique lifestyle experience by providing distinctive guest services, Schrager has created a new set of rules in hotel living that is not only emulated around the globe, but also conveyed in his new residential projects such as 40 Bond.

Der berühmte Lifestyle-Visionär Ian Schrager hat das Reisen mit völlig neuartigen Konzepten für die Hotelindustrie und Gastronomie revolutioniert. Seine Karriere begann in den Siebzigern, als er gemeinsam mit seinem damaligen Geschäftspartner Steve Rubell das legendäre Studio 54 gründete. Sein erstes Designhotel schuf er Mitte der Achtziger. Hierfür entwickelte er das Konzept des „Urban Resorts", einer Stadtoase, in dem die Gäste die Hauptattraktion darstellen. Schrager baute sieben weitere Hotels und schuf so das Vorbild für das heute allgegenwärtige Boutiquehotel. In Zusammenarbeit mit Künstlern wie Julian Schnabel und Philippe Starck entwickelte er ein einzigartiges Design und kreierte mit seinem herausragenden Servicekonzept einen einmaligen Stil. So ist es Schrager gelungen, neue Maßstäbe für das Leben im Hotel zu setzen, die weltweit nachgeahmt werden und auch in seinen neuen Wohnprojekten, wie 40 Bond, zu finden sind.

ER

Célèbre visionnaire du chic, Ian Schrager a modernisé notre façon de voyager par ses concepts révolutionnaires de l'industrie hôtelière. Il a d'abord a commencé sa carrière dans les années 1970 avec son associé Steve Rubell, aujourd'hui décédé, sur le légendaire Studio 54 avant de concevoir le premier hôtel design au milieu des années 1980. Son concept de « urban resort » fait du client l'attraction vedette des espaces publiques. Schrager a récidivé avec sept autres hôtels, aboutissant au modèle de l'hôtel-boutique omniprésent. Collaborant avec des artistes comme Julian Schnabel ou Philippe Starck pour créer un design original, et cultivant une expérience unique de ce style de vie par l'offre d'un service particulier aux clients, Schrager a créé un nouvel ensemble de règles hôtelières qui est non seulement mondialement imité, mais qui s'exprime aussi dans ses nouveaux projets résidentiels comme 40 Bond.

Un aura de visionario le rodea: Ian Schrager ha modernizado el modo en que viajamos con su revolucionaria concepción del negocio de la hostelería. Comenzó su carrera con el legendario Studio 54 junto a su socio Steve Rubell, ya fallecido, antes de poner en marcha su primer hotel de diseño a mediados de los 80, en el que los huéspedes en las zonas comunes eran la principal atracción. Schrager ha completado otros siete hoteles y ha cimentado en el proceso el patrón de los ahora ubicuos boutique hotels. A través de su colaboración con artistas como Julian Schnabel y Philippe Starck, ha creado una serie de diseños únicos y cultiva una experiencia única mediante los característicos servicios que ofrece a los huéspedes: Schrager ha creado también una nueva serie de normas de alojamiento en hoteles emuladas no sólo en todo el mundo, sino practicadas en sus nuevos proyectos residenciales, como 40 Bond.

BOWERY HOTEL AND GEMMA RESTAURANT

The burgeoning music and art scene of the East Village is the perfect location for this bohemian-like hotel with opulent touches of Persian rugs on the floors, a cluster of antlers on the walls and velvet seating. With just 135-rooms and suites of contrasting interiors that sway from hunting lodge to Victorian Gothic, this boutique hotel brings the stylish set back to a new kind of Old New York design.

Die boomende Musik- und Kunstszene des East Village ist der perfekte Standort für dieses unkonventionelle Hotel, in dem ein Hauch von Opulenz – Perserteppiche auf den Böden, Geweihe an den Wänden und samtbezogene Sessel – den Ton bestimmt. Mit insgesamt 135 individuell gestalteten Zimmern und Suiten – von der Jagdhütte bis hin zum viktorianischen Gothic-Zimmer – gelingt es dem Boutiquehotel, stylische Modernität in eine neue Interpretation des alten New Yorker Stils einzubringen.

La scène artistique et musicale en plein essor de l'East Village est l'endroit parfait pour cet hôtel au look bohémien avec la touche opulente de ses tapis persans au sol, sa collection de bois de cerf aux murs et ses sièges de velours. Avec exactement 135 chambres et suites aux intérieurs contrastés allant du pavillon de chasse au style gothique victorien, cet hôtel-boutique pousse le style décontracté vers une nouvelle sorte de design new-yorkais vieillot.

El bullicioso ambiente musical y artístico de East Village es el emplazamiento perfecto para este bohemio hotel y sus opulentos toques decorativos: alfombras persas en los pasillos, cornamentas en las paredes y sillas y asientos de terciopelo. Sus 135 habitaciones y suites recorren un amplio espectro de la decoración de interiores, desde el estilo noble y rural hasta el gótico victoriano, que retrotrae a la clientela de este coqueto hotel a otras épocas en el diseño del viejo nueva York.

BOWERY HOTEL

335 Bowery // Bowery
Tel.: +1 212 505 1300
www.theboweryhotel.com

6 to Bleecker St or F, V to 2nd Ave Lower East Side

GEMMA TRATTORIA

335 Bowery // Bowery
Tel.: +1 212 505 9100
www.theboweryhotel.com

Mo–Fri 7 am to noon (breakfast), noon to 4 pm (lunch),
Sun–Wed 4 pm to midnight, Thur–Sat to 1 am (dinner),
Sat–Sun 7 am to 10.30 am (breakfast),
10.30 am to 4 pm (brunch)

CROSBY STREET HOTEL

SIMONE

Each of the 86 rooms in the Crosby Street Hotel were individually designed by Kit Kemp with an eye towards clever combinations of color and texture and the seamless melding of modern and antique pieces. The colorful and eclectic interior fosters a quirky yet cozy appeal and original artwork placed throughout the hotel adds a unique edge. As all of the building materials are sustainable and energy-efficient, the Crosby Street Hotel is the epitome of "green luxury."

Die 86 Räume wurden individuell von Kit Kemp gestaltet – mit viel Gefühl für ausgesuchte Farb- und Materialkombinationen und einer gelungenen Mischung aus modernen und alten Elementen. Das farbenfrohe, vielseitige Interieur schafft eine ausgefallene, aber gemütliche Atmosphäre, und die im ganzen Gebäude ausgestellten Kunstwerke verleihen dem Hotel seinen einzigartigen Charakter. Alle verwendeten Baustoffe sind umweltverträglich und energiesparend – somit ist das Crosby Street Hotel die Krönung des „grünen Luxus".

Chacune des 86 chambres du Crosby Street Hotel a été individuellement imaginée par Kit Kemp dont l'œil s'exprime dans les choix habiles de couleur et de texture et le mélange naturel de pièces modernes et anciennes. L'intérieur chamarré et éclectique adopte un style excentrique mais chaleureux et des œuvres originales placées partout dans l'hôtel apportent une touche unique. Comme tout le bâtiment est de haute qualité environnementale et économe en énergie, cet hotel est l'incarnation du « luxe écolo ».

Cada una de las 86 habitaciones del Crosby Street Hotel fue diseñada por Kit Kemp para combinar con acierto colores y texturas y vincular a la perfección las piezas clásicas y modernas. El interior colorista y eclético potencia su atractivo, desacostumbrado pero acogedor, y el arte original que lo adorna le da carácter. Todos los materiales de construcción son sostenibles y de alta eficiencia energética, lo que hace del establecimiento el epítome del "lujo verde".

CROSBY STREET HOTEL

79 Crosby Street // SoHo
Tel.: +1 212 226 6400
www.firmdale.com

R, W to Prince St Station or 6 to Spring St Station

As the tallest building in the area, the Hotel on Rivington boasts unparalleled views of Manhattan seen through the floor-to-ceiling windows that comprise the building's monochromatic and modern facade. The hotel's entrance, a futuristic, egg-shaped tunnel designed by industrial designer Marcel Wanders, pays homage to the creative energy of the Lower East Side. The resident restaurant Thor compliments the airy nature of the hotel with a sleek, modern design and a large skylight.

Als das höchste Gebäude der Gegend bietet das Hotel mit raumhohen Fenstern, die sich zu einer monochromen modernen Fassade zusammensetzen, einzigartige Ausblicke auf Manhattan. Betreten wird das Hotel durch einen futuristisch anmutenden eierförmigen Tunnel – entworfen von Industriedesigner Marcel Wanders – eine Hommage an die kreative Energie der Lower East Side. Das Restaurant Thor vervollständigt mit seinem puren, modernen Design und einem großen Oberlicht den luftigen Charakter des Hotels.

Étant le plus grand bâtiment du quartier, The Hotel on Rivington offre des vues incomparables de Manhattan au travers des fenêtres toute hauteur qui composent la façade monochrome et moderne du bâtiment. Le hall de l'hôtel, un tunnel ovoïde futuriste conçu par le designer industriel Marcel Wanders, rend hommage à l'énergie créatrice de la Lower East Side. Le restaurant du Thor complète le caractère spacieux de l'hôtel par son design élégant et moderne et sa grande verrière.

Edificio más alto de la zona, el Hotel on Rivington ofrece incomparables vistas de Manhattan desde los altísimos ventanales que conforman la moderna y monocromática fachada del edificio. El acceso al establecimiento es un túnel aovado concebido por el diseñador industrial Marcel Wanders que rinde homenaje a la energía creativa del Lower East Side. El restaurante Thor, sito en el propio hotel, complementa la espaciosa naturaleza de este con un diseño moderno y elegante y un inmenso lucernario.

HOTEL ON RIVINGTON

107 Rivington Street // Lower East Side
Tel.: +1 212 475 2600
www.hotelonrivington.com

F, J, M, Z to Essex St / Delancey

THE GREENWICH HOTEL + LOCANDA VERDE

Despite being a fairly recent addition to the area, the Greenwich Hotel looks like it has been there since the turn of the century. Décor and furnishings drawn from a vast range of cultural influences and eras add to the understated elegance of the hotel. Of the 88 guest rooms, no two are exactly alike in design, enhancing the detail to craftsmanship and relaxed atmosphere that permeate the space.

Obwohl das Greenwich Hotel ein relativer Neuzugang im Viertel ist, wirkt es, als sei es schon seit Beginn des letzten Jahrhunderts dort ansässig. Dekor und Mobiliar lassen eine Vielzahl unterschiedlicher Kultureinflüsse und Epochen erkennen und tragen zum eleganten Understatement des Hotels bei. Keines der 88 Hotelzimmer gleicht einem anderen – gemeinsam sind ihnen jedoch detailgenaue Handwerkskunst und eine überall spürbare entspannte Atmosphäre.

Bien que d'addition tardive au quartier, le Greenwich semble avoir été là depuis le début du siècle. Le décor et l'ameublement inspirés d'un large éventail d'influences culturelles et de styles variés renforce l'élégance raffinée de l'hôtel. Sur les 88 chambres il n'en existe pas deux identiques, ce qui met en valeur les détails talentueux des artistes et l'atmosphère décontractée qui imprègnent l'espace.

Pese a su aparición relativamente reciente en la zona, el Greenwich Hotel da la impresión de haber estado ahí desde comienzos del siglo XX. La decoración y el mobiliario beben de una amplia variedad de fuentes culturales y eras y cimientan la sutil elegancia del establecimiento. En ninguna de las 88 habitaciones se repite el diseño, lo que refuerza el aire artesanal y relajado que permea el hotel.

THE GREENWICH HOTEL

377 Greenwich Street // TriBeCa
Tel.: +1 212 941 8900
www.thegreenwichhotel.com

1 to Franklin St or A, C, E to Canal St

LOCANDA VERDE

377 Greenwich Street // TriBeCa
Tel.: +1 212 925 3797
www.locandaverdenyc.com

Mo–Fr 8 am to 11 am (breakfast), 11.30 am to 3 pm (lunch),
Mo–Sun 5.30 pm to 11 pm (dinner),
Sat–Sun 8 am to 10 am (breakfast), 10 am to 3 pm (brunch)

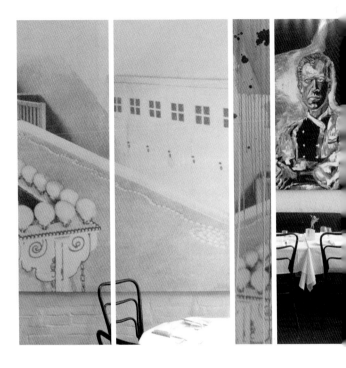

WALLSÉ RESTAURANT

344 West 11th Street // West Village
Tel.: +1 212 352 2300
www.wallserestaurant.com

Mon–Sun 5 pm to 11 pm, Sat–Sun 11 am to 2.30 pm
1 to Christopher St Sheridan Sq or A, C, E, L to 8th Ave 14th St

In an effort to highlight the Austrian cuisine served at Wallsé, the décor is intentionally chaste and subdued. Yet the white walls, black banquettes and handmade light fixtures in the dining room subtly hint at the Art Nouveau style, seamlessly creating a contemporary aesthetic. The experience is heightened by the private collection of artist and filmmaker Julian Schnabel that adorns the restaurant's walls.

Ausstattung und Dekor des Wallsé sind bewusst schlicht und dezent gehalten – so wird die österreichische Küche in den Mittelpunkt gerückt. Dennoch spielen weiße Wände, schwarze Bänke und handgefertigte Lampen im Speiseraum geschickt auf den Jugendstil an und erschaffen so mühelos eine zeitgemäße Ästhetik. Dieses besondere Flair wird durch die an den Wänden des Restaurants ausgestellte Privatsammlung des Künstlers und Filmemachers Julian Schnabel noch gesteigert.

Afin de promouvoir la cuisine autrichienne qui y est servie, le décor du Wallsé est volontairement sobre et soumis. Pourtant, les murs blancs, les banquettes noires et les éclairages artisanaux de la salle suggèrent le style Art Nouveau, créant imperceptiblement une esthétique contemporaine. Cette sensation est renforcée par la présence de la collection privée de l'artiste et cinéaste Julian Schnabel qui orne les murs du restaurant.

La decoración voluntariamente modesta y escueta del establecimiento pretende que la atención se centre sobre la excelencia de la cocina austríaca que en él se sirve. Aun así, las paredes blancas, los negros bancos y los apliques artesanales del comedor evocan sutilmente el estilo modernista y completan una estética contemporánea y sin fisuras. La experiencia se complementa con la colección privada del artista y cineasta Julian Schnabel que adorna las paredes del restaurante.

GRIFFOU

21 West 9th Street // Greenwich Village
Tel.: +1 212 358 0228
www.griffou.com

Mon–Sun 6 pm to 11.45 pm
A, B, C, D, E, F, V to W 4th St Station
or R, W to 8th St NYU Station

This intimate underground restaurant resides in an old Greenwich Village townhouse with six connected rooms that are styled with different contrasting themes that change seasonally. The restaurant interiors are laden with curiosities and antiquities from taxidermy to hunting gear and vintage portraits to weathered wood tables, conjuring up images of a centuries-old hunting lodge belonging to European aristocracy.

Dieses intime unterirdische Restaurant befindet sich in einem alten Townhouse in Greenwich Village. Jeder der sechs miteinander verbundenen Räume ist individuell gestaltet wobei das Dekorationsthema saisonal wechselt. Das Interieur des Restaurants besticht durch Kuriositäten und Antiquitäten – von ausgestopften Tieren bis zu Jagdausrüstungen, von alten Porträtbildern bis zu verwitterten Holztischen. So entsteht eine Atmosphäre, die an eine Jahrhunderte alte Jagdhütte eines britischen Aristokraten erinnert.

Ce restaurant chaleureux en sous-sol se trouve dans une ancienne maison de Greenwich Village, où six pièces communicantes sont décorées de thèmes variés et contrastés qui changent suivant la saison. Les intérieurs du restaurant sont chargés de curiosités et d'antiquités, des animaux empaillés aux armes de chasse, des portraits d'époque aux tables en bois usées, évoquant les images d'un antique pavillon de chasse appartenant à l'aristocratie britannique.

Intimista restaurante alojado en un viejo edificio de Greenwich Village, con seis habitaciones interconectadas y decoradas en temas contrastivos que cambian con las estaciones. El interior del restaurante está cargado de curiosidades y antigüedades, desde animales disecados a útiles de caza, retratos antiguos y baqueteadas mesas de madera que evocan las centenarias salas de cazadores de la aristocracia británica.

D

Designer Ichiro Sato based the overall concept of the interiors on the traditional Japanese home with authentic antique wood panels with a modern Tokyo aesthetic. Oversized windows, soaring ceilings, open kitchen, private dining areas, and dramatic Japanese-style centerpiece provide a beautiful backdrop for the izakaya-style dining served here.

Für das Gesamtkonzept des Interieurs ließ sich Designer Ichiro Sato von traditionellen japanischen Wohnhäusern inspirieren. Echt antike Holzpanelen treffen auf eine moderne Tokioer Ästhetik. Übergroße Fenster, hohe Decken, offene Küche, abgetrennte private Esszimmer und ein dramatisch anmutendes zentrales Designstück im japanischen Stil bieten ein perfektes Ambiente für die hier angebotenen Izakaya-inspirierten Speisen.

Le designer Ichiro Sato a basé tout le concept de cet intérieur sur la maison japonaise traditionnelle avec d'authentiques panneaux antiques de bois dans une esthétique tokyoïte moderne. Des fenêtres surdimensionnées, des hauts plafonds, une cuisine ouverte, des alcôves privées et une sculpture centrale dramatique de style japonais fournissent

El diseñador Ichiro Sato basó el concepto general interiorismo en el hogar tradicional japonés, con auténticos paneles de madera antigua y una estética tokyota moderna. Grandes ventanales, altísimos techos, una cocina abierta, comedores privados y una llamativa pieza central japonesa aportan el marco ideal para la cocina izakaya que sirve el estableci-

EN JAPANESE BRASSERIE

435 Hudson Street // TriBeCa
Tel.: +1 212 647 9196
www.enjb.com

Mon–Sat 12 pm to 2.30 pm (lunch),
Sun–Thur 5.30 pm to 11 pm,
Fri–Sat 5.30 pm to 12 am (dinner)
1 to Houston St Station

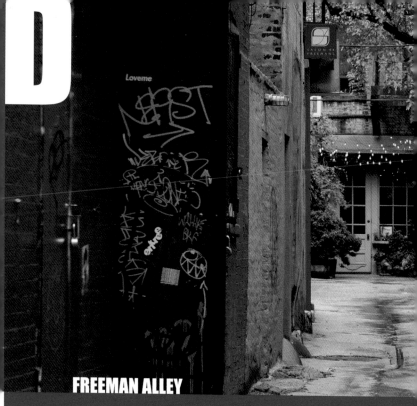

FREEMAN ALLEY

Located in a cozy space at the end of a non-descript alley near the Bowery, Freemans epitomizes the rugged, clandestine aesthetic of a colonial American tavern. The elusive location is emphasized by a series of small rooms that compose the space, each adorned with taxidermy and deftly scuffed floors. In the same tradition, Freemans Sporting Club and F.S.C. Barber Shop ooze masculine cool. It was established to honor the disappearing art of handmade, American garments and sells a refined collection of men's apparel.

Ein enger Platz in einer unauffälligen Seitengasse der Bowery: Hier steht das Freemans, Verkörperung der schroffen Ästhetik einer amerikanischen Kolonialtaverne. Die abgelegene Lage wird durch viele kleine Zimmer betont – dekoriert mit ausgestopften Tieren und abgewetzten Böden. Der Freemans Sporting Club und der F.S.C. Barber Shop strotzen ebenso vor cooler Maskulinität. Hier gibt es eine ausgesuchte Herrenkollektion in der verschwindenden Tradition handgemachter amerikanischer Kleidung.

Situé dans un espace confortable au fond d'une allée quelconque près du Bowery, Freemans incarne l'esthétique robuste et clandestine d'une taverne coloniale américaine. Ce lieu indéfinissable est composé d'une série de petites pièces, chacune agrémentée de taxidermie et de planchers trop facilement rayés. Dans le même genre, le FSC et son salon de coiffure transpirent la hype masculine. Créé pour honorer la disparition de l'artisanat et des vêtements américains, il vend une ligne raffinée de vêtements masculins.

Ubicado en un acogedor local al fondo de una anodina calleja cercana al Bowery, Freemans define a la perfección la estética descuidada y clandestina de las tabernas coloniales americanas. Las criaturas disecadas y suelos hábilmente desgastados de sus salas subrayan su carácter no necesariamente acogedor. El mismo estilo ultramasculino exudan el Freemans Sporting Club y la barbería, establecidos para salvaguardar el arte de la confección artesanal: allí se vende una refinada colección de moda masculina.

FREEMANS RESTAURANT

191 Chrystie Street // Lower East Side
End of Freeman Alley off Rivington betw. Bowery and Chrystie St
Tel.: +1 212 420 0012
www.freemansrestaurant.com

Mon–Fri 11 am to 4 pm (lunch), Sat–Sun 10 am to 4 pm (brunch),
Mon – Sun 6 pm to 11.30 pm (dinner)
J, M to Bowery Station or F, V to 2nd Ave Lower East Side Station

FREEMANS SPORTING CLUB
+ BARBER SHOP

8 Rivington Street // Lower East Side
Tel.: +1 212 673 3209
www.freemanssportingclub.com

Mon–Fri 12 am to 8 pm, Sat 11 am to 8 pm,
Sun 12 am to 6 pm

APPLE STORE FIFTH AVENUE

767 Fifth Avenue // Midtown
Tel.: +1 212 336 1440
www.apple.com/retail/fifthavenue

Open 24 hrs 7 days a week
N, R, W to 5th Ave Station

The 32-ft glass cube that serves as the entrance to the flagship Apple store on Fifth Avenue personifies the company's reputation for clever design and their "think different" motto. Upon entering the aboveground cube, customers choose a circular staircase or cylindrical glass elevator to descend onto the subterranean store floor where the latest Apple products are laid out on long, farmhouse-style tables. The store is also open 24/7 in recognition of the "city that never sleeps" reputation.

Betreten wird der Apple Flagship Store auf der 5th Avenue durch einen 10 m hohen Glaswürfel, der den Ruf des Unternehmens für gutes Design und dessen Motto „think different" verkörpert. Kunden betreten den Würfel und gelangen über eine runde Treppe oder mit dem zylinderförmigen Glasaufzug in die unterirdischen Geschäftsräume. Dort werden neuste Apple-Produkte auf langen rustikalen Tischen präsentiert. Als Hommage an die Stadt, die nie schläft, ist der Store täglich rund um die Uhr geöffnet.

Le cube vitré de 10 m qui sert d'entrée au magasin phare d'Apple sur la Cinquième Avenue incarne sa devise « Think different » et sa réputation pour le design malin. En entrant dans le cube au-dessus du sol, les clients choisissent entre un escalier circulaire et un ascenseur vitré cylindrique pour descendre au magasin souterrain où les derniers produits Apple sont présentés sur de longues tables de ferme. Le magasin est également ouvert en permanence en honneur de la « ville qui ne dort jamais ».

El cubo acristalado de diez metros de lado que abre el acceso a la tienda insignia de Apple en la Quinta Avenida recoge a la perfección la pasión por el diseño innovador de la empresa y su lema principal: "Think different". Tras acceder al cubo en la superficie, el cliente puede optar por una escalera de caracol o un ascensor cilíndrico para llegar a la tienda subterránea, donde los últimos productos de Apple aparecen expuesto en largas mesas rústicas. Como corresponde a la "ciudad que nunca duerme", la tienda no cierra nunca sus puertas.

Originally founded as a space for alternative arts, today Printed Matter has become the world's largest non-profit organization devoted to the appreciation, promotion and publication of artists' books. With over 15,000 books, fanzines and posters by 5,000 international artists on hand, the space in the Chelsea gallery district promotes the books themselves as works of art that serve as the voice of the ever-changing landscape of the contemporary art market.

Ursprünglich war das Printed Matter als Raum für alternative Kunst gedacht. Heute ist daraus die weltweit größte Non-Profit-Organisation geworden, die sich ganz der Anerkennung, Förderung und Verbreitung von Künstlerbüchern verschrieben hat. Über 15 000 Bücher, Fanzines und Poster von internationalen Künstlern werden hier angeboten. Printed Matter verschafft damit Büchern als eigenständigen Kunstwerken eine Stimme in der sich ständig wandelnden Landschaft des zeitgenössischen Kunstmarkts.

Fondée à l'origine comme un espace pour les arts alternatifs, Printed Matter est devenue aujourd'hui la plus grande organisation mondiale à but non lucratif consacrée à l'appréciation, la promotion et la publication de livres d'artistes. Détenant plus de 15 000 livres, de fanzines et d'affiches de 5 000 artistes internationaux, cet espace présente les livres comme étant eux-mêmes des œuvres d'art servant de voix au paysage toujours changeant du marché de l'art contemporain.

Creado originalmente como un espacio para las artes alternativas, en la actualidad Printed Matter se ha convertido en la organización altruista más grande del mundo dedicada a la apreciación, promoción y publicación de libros de arte libros de artistas. Con un catálogo de más de 15.000 volúmenes , fanzines y carteles de 5.000 artistas internacionales, este espacio promociona los libros como obras de arte de pleno derecho, la voz del paisaje siempre cambiante del mercado de arte contemporáneo.

PRINTED MATTER

195 10th Avenue // Chelsea
Tel.: +1 212 925 0325
www.printedmatter.org
www.nyartbookfair.com

Tue–Wed 11 am to 6 pm, Thur–Sat 11 am to 7 pm
C, E to 23rd St

VITRA

29 9th Avenue // Meatpacking District
Tel.: +1 212 463 5750
www.vitra.com

Mon–Sat 11 am to 7 pm, Sun 12 pm to 6 pm
A, C, E, L to 8th Ave 14th St

Designer furniture of museum quality takes center stage in this ultra-sleek, minimalist store. This international company is renowned for creating the most inspiring and creative furniture with some of the world's most sought-after designers, such as Frank Gehry, Charles and Ray Eames and Hella Jongerius, using top-notch Swiss manufacturing.

In diesem durchgestylten, minimalistischen Laden stehen Designmöbel in Museumsqualität im Mittelpunkt. Das internationale Unternehmen ist bekannt für seine höchst inspirierten und kreativen Möbelstücke, hier wird mit einigen der weltweit begehrtesten Designern zusammengearbeitet, wie zum Beispiel Frank Gehry, Charles und Ray Eames und Hella Jongerius. Immer dabei: Beste schweizerische Handwerkskunst.

Le mobilier design digne d'un musée est au centre de ce magasin minimaliste et ultraélégant. Cette entreprise internationale est réputée pour créer les meubles les plus ravissants et innovants avec la collaboration des designers les plus recherchés du monde, tels que Frank Gehry, Charles & Ray Eames et Hella Jongerius, et l'aide de fabricants suisses de tout premier ordre.

El mobiliario de diseño tiene una importancia fundamental en estas minimalistas tienen una, epítome de la elegancia. La compañía es famosa por producir los muebles más inspirados y creativos junto con los diseñadores más solicitados del momento, como Frank Gehry, Charles y Ray Eames y Hella Jongerius, y por fabricarlos con la insuperable calidad suiza.

The Prada store in SoHo is the ultimate union of famed architect Rem Koolhaas and the fashion powerhouse. Koolhaas took the 23,000 square feet of retail space and transformed it into a museum-worthy stage for the merchandise, designing a wooden "wave" at the center of the space that can be used for displays, performances, shows, and events.

Der Prada Store in SoHo ist das jüngste Gemeinschaftsprojekt von Stararchitekt Rem Koolhaas und dem dynamischen Modehaus. Koolhaas verwandelte die 2100 m² große Verkaufsfläche in eine museumsartige Bühne für die Ware, indem er eine „Holzwelle" in der Mitte des Raumes schuf, die für Auslagen, Performances, Shows und Events genutzt werden kann.

Le magasin Prada à SoHo est la rencontre ultime du célèbre architecte Rem Koolhaas et de géant de la mode. Koolhaas a transformé les 2 100 m² d'espace de vente en une scénographie digne d'un musée de la marchandise, imaginant une « vague » de bois au centre de l'espace, pouvant être utilisée pour des expositions, des happenings, des défilés et autres événements.

La tienda que Prada tiene en SoHo es la colaboración definitiva entre el arquitecto Rem Koolhaas y la prestigiosa casa de moda. Koolhaas ha transformado los 2 100 m² del espacio de ventas en un escenario, casi una sala de exposiciones de la mercancía, y en la que destaca una "ola" de madera en el centro que puede ser utilizada para presentaciones, actuaciones, espectáculos y eventos.

PRADA SOHO

575 Broadway // SoHo
Tel.: +1 212 334 8888
www.prada.com

Mon–Wed 11 am to 7 pm, Thur 11 am to 8 pm,
Fri – Sat 11 am to 7 pm, Sun 12 pm to 7 pm
R to Prince St Station or B, D, F, V to
Broadway-Lafayette St Station

MOSS GALLERY

150 Greene Street // SoHo
Tel.: +1 212 204 7100
www.mossonline.com

Mon–Sat 11 am to 7 pm
R to Prince St Station or B, D, F, V to Broadway-Lafayette St Station

Through carefully curated exhibitions, Moss is known to connect the unique relationships between various disciplines of design, art, function, and decoration by diminishing borders between craft and production, industrial design and decorative arts. Popular for its risk-taking approach to art exhibition, Moss showcases product design and furnishings as conceptual art form with the likes of such artists as Maarten Baas, Campana Brothers, Tord Boontje, and Tom Dixon, to name a few.

Die Moss Gallery ist für sorgfältig kuratierte Ausstellungen bekannt, welche die Grenzen zwischen angewandten und schönen Künsten auflösen: Handwerk und maschinelle Produktion, dekorative Künste und Industriedesign stellen keine Gegensätze mehr dar. Die Galerie stellt Produktdesignstücke und Möbel von Designer wie Maarten Baas, den Campana-Brüdern, Tord Boontje oder Tom Dixon aus als wären sie Konzeptkunst.

À l'aide d'expositions soigneusement organisées, Moss est devenu réputé pour ses connexions interdisciplinaires entre design, art, fonction et décoration grâce à la réduction des frontières entre artisanat et production, design industriel et arts décoratifs. Apprécié pour son approche risquée de l'exposition artistique, Moss met en valeur la conception des produits et le mobilier en tant que formes d'art conceptuel avec des artistes tels que Maarten Baas, Tord Boontje et

A través de sus minuciosamente organizadas exhibiciones, Moss se ha hecho famoso por evidenciar las singulares relaciones entre las distintas disciplinas del diseño, el arte, la función y la decoración difuminando los límites entre creación y producción, diseño industrial y artes decorativas. Conocido por sus arriesgadas exposiciones, Moss presenta el diseño industrial y el mobiliario como una forma de arte conceptual, ejemplificado por artistas como Maarten Baas, Tord Boontje

D

Famous for his unusual fabric creations and strange contouring patterns, it would only be fitting that the experimental Japanese fashion designer Issey Miyake would appoint Frank Gehry and Gordon Kipping to unleash his creative genius on his flagship store in Tribeca. From the 25-ft-high titanium twisting column aptly named "The Tornado" to the glass floors looking into the private showroom downstairs, there is always a sense of playfulness and discovery in this renovated landmark building.

Bekannt ist der Modedesigner Issey Miyake für phantasievolle Stoffkreationen und ungewöhnliche Schnittmuster. Passend also, dass er für seinen Flagship-Store auf die kreative Genialität von Frank Gehry und Gordon Kipping setzte. Von der über sieben m hohen gewundenen Titaniumsäule „Der Tornado" bis hin zu Glasböden, die Einblicke in private Showrooms im Untergeschoss ermöglichen – ein Gefühl von Verspieltheit und Abenteuerlust ist in diesem renovierten denkmalgeschützten Gebäude überall zu spüren.

Célèbre pour ses créations en tissu inhabituelles et ses motifs aux contours étranges, rien n'était plus tendance pour le concepteur de mode Issey Miyake que de nommer Frank Gehry et Gordon Kipping pour libérer son génie créateur dans le magasin phare. La colonne torsadée en titane de plus de sept mètres de haut, la bien nommée « The Tornado », comme les sols transparents donnant dans le magasin privé du bas, incitent au jeu et à la découverte toujours présents dans ce bâtiment historique rénové.

Famoso por sus extravagantes telas y desacostumbrados patrones, resulta apropiado que el diseñador de moda Issey Miyake recurriese a Frank Gehry y Gordon Kipping para que diesen rienda suelta a su creatividad en su tienda insignia. Desde la retorcida columna de titanio de siete metros de alto (apodada The Tornado) hasta los suelos acristalados abiertos al showroom privado de la planta inferior, la sensación de aventura y divertimento está siempre presente en este emblemático edificio renovado.

TRIBECA ISSEY MIYAKE

119 Hudson Street // TriBeCa
Tel.: +1 212 226 0100
www.tribecaisseymiyake.com

Mon–Sat 11 am to 7 pm, Sun 12 pm to 6 pm
1 to Franklin St or A, C, E to Canal St

UPTOWN

Uptown is not only the most heavily visited area of all of Manhattan with its ornate architecture, designer boutiques, and fine restaurants, but is celebrated for having the most important world class museums and cultural institutions in the city.

GRAMERCY

With its diverse architectural structures and immaculate streets, the mostly residential neighborhood surrounding Gramercy Park is considered a peaceful and lush oasis in the middle of the Manhattan concrete jungle.

MEATPACKING DISTRICT/
WEST VILLAGE/CHELSEA

Meatpacking District is a wholesale market by day and a super trendy bar and club area by night. Originally the bohemian capital of the country, the West Village is considered today a hub for the über-creative set and is

ART

ARCHITECTURE

MAP 157

most prized for its entertainment options. For those intent on a more happening art scene, Chelsea has over three hundred galleries in what has been labeled as the global center for contemporary art.

EAST VILLAGE/UNION SQUARE

Known for its artistic community, funky shops, and thriving nightlife, the East Village also has the highest number of bars in New York City. As the name suggests, Union

DESIGN

Square is the best meeting place in the city with its endless transportation options, but it's the place to meet up with the city's top chefs buying seasonal specialties at its famous open-air Greenmarket.

SOHO/TRIBECA

Once home to artists who favored the spacious industrial lofts for creating and displaying their works, Soho today is one of the most vibrant shopping areas in the city. Tribeca is a haven for sophisticated urbanites who appreciate the large warehouses and lofts in this former manufacturing district.

BOWERY/
LOWER EAST SIDE

With a great number of upscale condominiums erected in the recent decade catering to style-conscious professionals, both neighborhoods have been transformed from gritty to glamorous with an eclectic mix of funky bars, stylish restaurants, avant-garde fashion and rocking live-music venues.

BROOKLYN

Brooklyn is a vortex of creative activity where artists of all kinds can find inspiration. Williamsburg is one of the largest neighborhoods in Brooklyn yet has become the trendiest by appealing to the young hipster generation who appreciate its cultural diversity and large open spaces with low rents. The Dumbo district is a flourishing creative center with galleries and festivals celebrating various art forms.

UPPER
EST SIDE

16

BROADWAY

8

17

7

CENTRAL
PARK

5TH AVE

E 79th

5

4

3

2

E 88th

E 91st

E 86th

E 92th

PARK AVE

6

E 72th Str

UPPER
EAST SIDE

2ND AVE

1ST AVE

19

8

47

57TH STREET

2
21

MIDTOWN

FIRST AVE

ROOSEVELT
ISLAND

QUEENS-
BORO
BRIDGE

21ST STR

21ST STR.

46TH AVE

1

JACKSON AVE

QUEENS

PULASKI BRIDGE

BROOKLYN

EMERGENCY

Emergency number for Fire, Police, Ambulance Tel.: 911

ARRIVAL

BY PLANE

John F. Kennedy International Airport (JFK) 15 miles / 24 km east of the city center. National and international flights. Shuttle bus service or Air Train available into Midtown Manhattan. To take the Air Train or the subway into the city requires changing trains at either Howard Beach (to subway A) or Jamaica Station (to subway E, J, Z, or the Long Island Rail Road).

Newark Liberty International Airport (EWR) 16 miles / 26 km west of the city center. National and international flights. Newark Liberty Airport Express runs every 15 minutes to Manhattan (Port Authority Bus Terminal, Bryant Park, Grand Central Station).

www.panynj.gov -- for more airport information.

TOURIST INFORMATION

Official New York City Marketing and Tourism Organization
NYC & Company
810 Seventh Avenue
New York, NY 10019
Tel.: +1 212 484 1200
www.nycgo.com
Mon-Fri 8:30 am to 6 pm, Sat-Sun 9 am to 5 pm

New York Information Kiosks are located at: Whitehall Ferry Terminal (South of Battery Park), World Trade Center PATH Station (Church and Vesey Streets), NYC Heritage Tourism Center (Southern tip of City Hall Park on the Broadway sidewalk at Park Row), Chinatown (Triangle between Canal, Baxter, and Walker Streets)
www.nyc.gov – official website of New York City
www.iloveny.com – New York State Division of Tourism website
www.ny.com – comprehensive online tourist guide
www.nyc.gov/citymap – official city map

ACCOMMODATION

www.hotels.com – hotel booking service
www.nyhabitat.com – hotels, bed & breakfast, rooms, etc.

www.newyork.craigslist.org – insider tip for finding short-term sublets

www.priceline.com – hotel bookings with bidding feature

www.tripadvisor.com -- best hotel reviews with top value listing

TICKETS

www.ticketmaster.com – wide range of tickets for concerts, culture and sporting events, theater, and other events in New York City

www.tdf.org – discount tickets with reductions of 25%, 35% and 50% for Broadway and Off-Broadway shows, for dance performances and musicals

www.citypass.com – 50% entrance discount and no waiting times in the following locations: Empire State Building, MoMA, Guggenheim Museum, The Metropolitan Museum of Art and American Museum of Natural History as well as the 2-hour Circle Line boat tour

www.mta.info/metrocard – unlimited use of subway, Staten Island Railway and the city buses with the Unlimited Ride Metro-Card for one-day or 7-day tickets

GETTING AROUND

PUBLIC TRANSPORTATION

www.hopstop.com – online city transit guide

www.mta.info/nyct – Metropolitan Transportation Authority, Tel.: +1 718 330 1234

TAXI

Normally cabs can be stopped by waving the hand when the number on the roof is lighted. Use only yellow taxis that are licensed and equipped with a taxi meter. Taxi and Limousine Commission, Tel.: +1 212 302 8294

BICYCLE RENTALS

Rental bikes are available in various shops around Central Park, through several bike shop locations throughout the city, such as www.masterbikeshop.com, or Pier 84 along the Hudson River Greenway for www.bikeandroll.com. For a complete listing go online at www.bikenewyork.org under Local Info.

CAR RENTAL

Besides the international rental car companies, Zipcar rental agency is an online membership car club service that allows users to share cars either by the day or on an hourly basis from cars parked throughout the city – www.zipcar.com

CITY TOURS

LOCAL PUBLIC TRANSPORT

The most inexpensive way to tour Manhattan is with the M1 bus from East 8th Street/4th Avenue (Mon-Fri also from South Ferry) to West 146th Street in Harlem and back. Using the subway is another greatw way to explore the different neighborhoods all throughout Manhattan by stopping at major stations and traveling by foot.

SIGHTSEEING BUSES

www.graylinenewyork.com – uptown and downtown routes including specially themed tours such as the Holiday Lights Tour, Tel.: +1 212 445 0848

www.citysightsny.com – hop-on, hop-off double-decker bus tours, Tel.: +1 212 812 2700

www.newyorkpartyshuttle.com – OnBoard New York Sightseeing Tours, Tel.: +1 212 852 4821

BOAT TOURS

www.circleline42.com – Circle Line Sightseeing Cruises, Tel.: +1 212 563 3200

www.circlelinedowntown.com – Circle Line Downtown, Tel.: +1 212 269 5755

www.nywatertaxi.com – New York Water Taxi, Tel.: +1 212 742 1969

SIGHTSEEING FLIGHT TOURS

www.heliny.com – Helicopter Flight Services, Tel.: +1 212 355 0801

www.libertyhelicopters.com – Liberty Helicopter Tours, Tel.: +1 212 967 6464

GUIDED TOURS

www.bigapplegreeter.org – Big Apple Greeter, Tel.: +1 212 669 8159 – people from New York provide a free guided tour for visitors through their city

www.bigonion.com – Big Onion Walking Tours, Tel.: +1 888 606 9255 – competently guided walkabouts concentrating on special aspects and topics with themed tours

www.bikethebigapple.com – Bike the Big Apple, Tel.: +1 877 865 0078 – guided bike tours through New York that last from 5-7 hours

ART AND ARCHITECTURAL GUIDES TOURS

www.mas.org – Discover New York Walking Tours, Tel.: +1 212 439 1049 – sponsored by the Municipal Art Society, these tours are led by architectural and urban historians to explore neighborhoods

www.nycwalk.com – New York City Cultural Walking Tours, Tel.: +1 212 979 2388 – tours cover such diverse topics as gargoyles on buildings and the old Yiddish theaters of the East Village

www.artsmart.com – Art Smart Art Tours + Advisory, Tel.: +1 212 595 4444 – customized tours of museums and galleries as well as art-related travel programs for individuals or groups
www.arttoursnewyork.com – New York Art Tours, Tel.: +1 212 874 6627 – insider look at New York's art scene led by a professional art critic.

ART & CULTURE

www.nyc-arts.org – art events calendar
www.nyc.com/events – culture events calendar
www.new.york.eventguide.com – event guide
www.nymag.com/agenda – New York magazine culture calendar
www.artfaircalendar.com – calendar of art shows and fairs
www.artinfo.com/galleryguide – guide to galleries in New York
www.artincontext.org – museum guide (select up to region New York)
www.manyonline.org – Museum Association of New York
www.artcat.com – information on lesser known art shows and galleries
www.nyc-architecture.com – information on significant monuments in New York
www.nycgovparks.org – listing of all permanent art and monuments
www.playbill.com – Playbill's Official Website

GOING OUT

www.villagevoice.com – city's most popular city magazine with in-scene news
www.newyorktimes.com – event calendar, online ticket service, restaurant search engine and more city entertainment information online
www.nymag.com – covers the arts, entertainment, fashion and food as well as a special section that features what is happening weekly
www.timeoutny.com – the bible for entertainment in New York City

EVENTS

JANUARY TO MARCH

www.whitney.org – the Whitney Biennial is one of the leading annual exhibitions of contemporary art in the nation from February to May
www.artexponewyork.com – hosts the world's top artists at the world's largest fine art trade show
www.thearmoryshow.com – the highly acclaimed Armory Show is America's leading contemporary fine art fair
www.artdealers.org – the Art Show is organized by the Art Dealers Association of America with exhibitions from the nation's leading art galleries

www.scope-art.com – art fair introduces top artists, curators, and galleries with an international list of exhibitors from four continents

www.pulse-art.com – a four-day fair dedicated to contemporary art with a mix of established and emerging galleries

www.aipad.com – the AIPAD Photography Show New York features a wide range of photography from more than 70 leading art galleries

APRIL TO JUNE

www.haughton.com – the International Fine Art Fair brings together the world's top art dealers of paintings, drawings and sculpture at the Park Avenue Armory

www.tribecafilmfestival.org – an international film festival that takes place in spring every year in lower Manhattan

www.danceparade.org – honors the diversity of dance traditions with a parade showcasing 65 different dance forms

www.nyphotofestival.com – five-day event celebrating contemporary photography in New York's new photo district —Dumbo, Brooklyn

www.washingtonsquareoutdoorartexhibit.org – for two weekends in May and in September, this biannual juried festival showcases sculpture, photography and crafts from living artists today

JULY TO SEPTEMBER

www.museummilefestival.org – nine of America's best museums 82nd Street to 105th Street with entertainment and free access to all museums

www.nyc-arts.org – the River to River Festival takes place in Lower Manhattan with a host of free events taking place from June to August

www.lincolncenter.org – the Lincoln Center Festival hosts various dance, music, opera, circus and theater performances from around the world during July

www.summerstage.org – free performances by international artists and big name benefit shows on the main stage in Central Park and around the city from June to September

www.filmlinc.com – the coveted New York Film Festival takes place in the Lincoln Center in late September with cinematic works by filmmakers from around the world

OCTOBER TO DECEMBER

www.ohny.org – hosts year-round programs celebrating New York City's built environment ending with an annual weekend celebration as America's largest architecture and design event

www.ifpda.org – the IFPDA Print Fair focuses on fine prints from all periods and also hosts the week-long New York Fine Art Print Week

Cover photo (Museum of Modern Art) designed by Yoshio Taniguchi. Night view of The Abby Aldrich Rockefeller Sculpture Garden and The David and Peggy Rockefeller Building, photo by Timothy Hursley, courtesy of Museum of Modern Art

ART

p 10-13 (P.S.1) architecture by Frederick Fisher, p 10, 11 photo by Matthew Septimus, p 12, 13 photos by Claudia Hehr p 14 (Cooper-Hewitt Design Museum) and p 15 left photo by Dennis Cowley, Cooper-Hewitt Shop images by Harald T. Schreiber, right photo by Andrew Garn, all courtesy of Cooper-Hewitt Design Museum p 16, 17 (Solomon R. Guggenheim Museum) architecture by Frank Lloyd Wright, photos by Martin Nicholas Kunz (further mentioned as mnk) p 18, 19 (Neue Galerie New York Museum for German and Austrian Art), renovation designed by Annabelle Selldorf, p 18, 19 left, right photos by Claudia Hehr, middle courtesy of Neue Galerie New York Museum for German and Austrian Art p 20-23 (Metropolitan Museum of Art) photos by Claudia Hehr, p 20 right by mnk p 24-27 (Whitney Museum of American Art) p 24, 25, 27 photos by Claudia Hehr, p 26 by mnk p 28 (Museum of Arts and Design) middle by Hélène Binet, left and right, p 29 courtesy of Museum of Arts and Design p 32-35 (Museum of Modern Art), p 32, 33, 34 middle photos by Timothy Hursley, p 34 left and right, p 35 left and left middle (MoMA Shop) by Roland F. Bauer, middle courtesy of The Modern, middle right, right by Peter Hueber of ARCH photo, courtesy of The Modern p 36, 37 (International Center of Photography), architecture by Gwathmey Siegel & Associates Architects, photos by Paul Warhol p 38 (Gagosian Gallery) photo by Robert McKeever, p 39 by James McKee p 40 (Matthew Marks Gallery) photos courtesy of Matthew Marks Gallery New York, p 40 right and 41 artwork of Charles Ray p 42, 43 (Barbara Gladstone Gallery) photos by David Regen, courtesy of Barbara Gladstone Gallery

p 44-47 (New Museum), architecture by Kazuyo Sejima & Ryue Nishizawa, artwork p 44, 45, left to right: Pazuzu (2008) by Roberto Cuoghi, Pegged (1996) by Kara Walker, Fall '91, (1992) by Charles Ray; p 46 left Super Sister (1999) by Liza Lou, middle There is plenty of room at the bottom (2010) by Julieta Aranda, right Untitled (Bowed Woman) (1995) by Kiki Smith; except for the artwork by Julieta Aranda, all artwork is courtesy of DESTE Foundation from the collection of Dakis Joannou, photos by Lizzy Courage (further mentioned as lc), p 46 left middle, middle right, right and p 47 by mnk p 48 (Clic Bookstore & Gallery), p 49 left, middle photos by mnk, right by lc p 50, 51 (Wild Horses of Sable Island) artwork by Roberto Dutesco at www.dutescoart.com, photos by Robert DiScalfini, courtesy of Roberto Dustesco, copy courtesy of Richard Friswall

ARCHITECTURE

p 56 (Alice Tully Hall) original building 1969 by Pietro Belluschi, new architecture by Diller Scofidio + Renfro, photo by mnk, p 57 by Iwan Baan p 58 (Hearst Tower) architecture by Lord Norman Foster + Partners, photo left and right by mnk, middle courtesy of Hearst Corporation, p 59 by mnk p 60, 61 (Joan Weill Center for Dance, Alvin Ailey American Dance Theater) architecture by lu + Bibliowicz Architects LLP (2005), photos by ARCHphoto p 62 (Top of the Rock), architecture by Raymond Hood, photos by mnk, p 63 by Claudia Hehr p 64 (New York Times Building) architecture by Renzo Piano Building Workshop with FXFowle Architects, photos by Nic Lehoux, p 65 middle, right by David Sundberg p 66, 67 (Chrysler Building), architecture by William Van Alen, left, middle photos by Claudia Hehr, right by mnk; p 68, 69 (Grand Central Station) architecture by The Associated Architects of Grand Central Terminal (Reed & Stern, Warren & Wetmore), Beyer, Blinder & Belle (restoration, 1998), photos by mnk p 70, 71 (Morgan Library Expansion) architecture by Renzo Piano Building Workshop, photos by Michel Denancé p 72 (IAC Headquarters) architecture by Frank O. Gehry, left and middle photos by Albert Vecerka of Esto photographics, right, p 73 by mnk

p 74 (The Porter House) architecture by Gregg Pasquarelli of ShoP Architects, photos by Seong Kwon, p 75 by mnk

p 76-79 (The High Line) architecture by Diller Scofidio + Renfro, landscape design by James Corner Field Operations, photos by mnk

p 80, 81 (The Standard New York) architecture by Todd Schliemann of Polshek Partnership Architects, interior design by Roman & Williams, p 80, 81 middle right, right photos by Nikolas Koenig courtesy The Standard, left and left middle by mnk

p 82 (The Center for Architecture) architecture by Andrew Berman Architect, photos by Björn Wallander, p 83 by Roy Wright

p 84, 85 (Cooper Union School of Art) architecture by Thom Mayne of Morphosis, photos by mnk, renderings courtesy of Morphosis

p 86-89 (Cooper Square Hotel) architecture by Carlos Zapata Studio, interior design by Antonio Citterio and partners photos by mnk

p 90-93 (40 Bond) architecture by Herzog & de Meuron, p 92 bottom left by Iwan Baan, all others courtesy of Ian Schrager Company for 40 Bond

p 94, 95 (Blue Condominium) architecture by Bernard Tschumi Architects, p 94 and 95 left photos by mnk, right by Peter Mauss of Esto photographics

p 96, 97 (40 Mercer Residences) architecture by Jean Nouvel with SLCE Architects, architectural renderings by Advanced Media Design Inc, www.studioamd.com

p 98-101 (National September 11 Memorial and Museum) architecture by Michael Arad, landscape design by Peter Walker, renderings by Squared Design Lab

p 104, 105 (Skyscraper Museum) architecture by Skidmore, Owings & Merrill, photos by mnk

DESIGN

p 110, 111 (Room Mate Grace) designed by Lindy Roy, photos by mnk

p 112-115 (ACE Hotel) designed by Roman and Williams, p 112, 113 artwork by Morning Breath, p 114 left, left middle, middle, middle right,

p 115 right (The Breslin Bar & Dining Room) photos by mnk, p 114 right, p 115 (Stumptown Coffee Roasters) left, left middle and middle by lc

p 116, 117 (Gramercy Park Hotel) artwork and design by Julian Schnabel, photos courtesy of Gramercy Park Hotel

p 120-123 (Bowery Hotel) architecture by Scarano Architects, designed by Sean MacPherson, p 120, 121 photos courtesy of Bowery Hotel, others by mnk and lc

p 124-127 (Crosby Street Hotel) designed by Kit Kemp, p 124, 125, 126 and p 127 middle photos by mnk, left, left middle, middle right, right by lc

p 128, 129 (Hotel on Rivington) architecture by Grzywinski Pons, interior design by India Mondavi, restaurant Thor designed by Marcel Wanders, photos by mnk

p 130-133 (The Greenwich Hotel + Locanda Verde) designed by Grayling Design (public areas), Mikio Shinagawa (Shibui Spa)Samantha Crasco (rooms), photos by mnk and lc

p 134, 135 (Wallsé Restaurant) designed by Constantin Wickensburg Architects PC, Philip von Hohenlohe Consulting, Tirschwell & Co Inc. (lighting), photos by mnk

p 136, 137 (Griffou) architecture by Daniel O'Connor Architects, concept by Larry Poston, Johnny Swet and Jesse Keyes, photos by mnk

p 138, 139 (EN Japanese Brasserie) designed by Ichiro Sato, Kushner Studios, Age Design Ltd., photos by mnk

p 140, 141 (Freeman Alley), restaurant and FSC design concept by Taavo Somer and William Tigertt, p 142 (Freemans Restaurant) photos by mnk, p 143 (Freemans Sporting Club) left courtesy of Freemans Sporting Club, all others by lc

p 144, 145 (Apple Store Fifth Avenue) designed by Bohlin Cywinski Jackson, photos by Claudia Hehr

p 146, 147 (Printed Matter) photos by mnk and lc

p 148, 149 (Vitra) designed by Lindy Roy; photos by mnk and lc

p 150, 151 (Prada SoHo) designed by Rem Koolhaas, photos courtesy of Prada; p 152, 153 (Moss Gallery) photos by Roland F. Bauer

p 154, 155 (Tribeca Issey Miyake) designed by Frank O. Gehry, Gordon Kiping (sculpture/interiors), photos by mnk

PUBLISHED IN THE SAME SERIES

ISBN 978-3-8327-9433-0

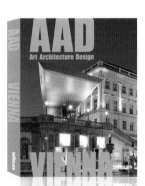

ISBN 978-3-8327-9434-7

UPCOMING TITLES

BARCELONA, LONDON + PARIS